The Solgohachia Murders
A Fryer Family Tragedy

Barton Jennings

The Solgohachia Murders: A Fryer Family Tragedy
Copyright © 2024 by Barton Jennings

All rights reserved. This book may not be duplicated or transmitted in any way, or stored in an information retrieval system, without the express written consent of the publisher, except in the form of brief excerpts or quotations for the purpose of review. Making copies of this book, or any portion, for any purpose other than your own, is a violation of United States copyright laws.

Publisher's Cataloging-in-Publication Data
Jennings, Barton

The Solgohachia Murders: A Fryer Family Tragedy
156p.; 21cm.
ISBN: 979-8-9904307-1-6
Library of Congress Control Number: 2024944528

Front cover photo from the collection of Tomme Jennings. This photo of Maye, Erdie and Abbie is from a better time before the shootings of April 26, 1915.
Cover background graphic: *130 Retro Book Covers* copyright ArtistMef (Ihor Vitkovskyi) via Creative Market.
Back cover photo by Sarah Jennings.

TechScribes, Inc.
PO Box 2199
Alma, AR 72921
www.techscribes.com

Printed in the United States of America

Contents

Acknowledgments	5
Introduction	9
The Fryer Family Prior to 1915	13
The Community of Solgohachia	23
Fryer's Ford Bridge	35
The Family Tragedy of April 26, 1915	45
The Trials and Years of Frustration	75
The Fryer Family Post-1915	109
About the Author	155

Dedication

For Erdie, Abbie, Dick and Amos –
and the survivors of that horrible night.

Acknowledgments

Probably most families have an event or story that has been kept secret over time. This one is mine. Stories like this can be hard to tell, especially when those involved never wanted to speak about it. Additionally, events of more than 100 years ago are often made hazy by legend, family stories, and sometimes not the most accurate reporting.

As was tradition within my family, and apparently other Solgohachia families, few spoke about the murders of April 26, 1915. What was said was never complete, generally just a brief outline with a warning to not repeat it, especially to those who were there that terrible evening. In-laws and friends sometimes heard parts of the story, especially when they were drawn into it through a chance encounter. However, all of the details were never shared. Therefore, the research will probably never be complete, and all of the details may never be known.

I have been fortunate to get some of the internal details from family members of the Fryer, Bearden and Gordon families. Several families in the Solgohachia and Morrilton areas have also included details about the shootings in their published histories, especially those that housed the survivors or knew them well. As always, there are conflicts in the various versions and some of the details are certainly wrong. Incorrect names and dates sometimes happen after being told time after time, but additional research using multiple sources has hopefully straightened most of these errors out.

Historic records of the Arkansas Supreme Court, the Caselaw Access Project of the Harvard Law School, *The Southwest Reporter*, and numerous articles from magazines, journals, and newspapers from across the country have provided much of the public side of the shootings, as well as the legal cases that followed. It has been amazing to find newspapers from coast to coast carrying articles about the events, but most seem to be copied from local articles, especially those in the *Arkansas Gazette* and *Arkansas Democrat* newspapers. A number of important articles with local sources were found in several area newspapers, including the weekly German-language newspaper *Das Arkansas Echo*. Here again, errors are found, some later corrected and some not.

With the Fryer and Bearden families apparently speaking little to reporters, the news stories tended to focus on the shooter and witnesses and not the suffering family members. Reading the various statements in these articles gives a feel for the emotions at the time, some that have remained for more than a century. They especially show Floy Maye Fryer growing up and taking the lead in the public defense of her family. I certainly understand my Aunt Toots (Maye) better by reading her statements from the time.

My mother, the youngest daughter of Gladys Fryer Wilson, has been the traffic cop of my research, making sure I have the Fryer family names straight (a huge challenge), passing on the family stories, and working through the many family photo albums that produced the historic photographs used in this book. Jerry Kathleen Fryer Rider and her daughter Dr. Jan Wilhite have been a big help in getting the stories involving Buddy Fryer, another survivor of that night. Other family members have also provided documentation and stories.

Documents from the Bearden family, especially the materials written by Joan Bearden Broening and obtained from the Morrilton Depot Museum and Genealogy Library, have also helped to fill in some of the details. Thankfully, a tour of the sites in Solgohachia was provided by John Gordon, who's family was involved with the court case and still lives in the area.

Several organizations made available historical files and archives, government and court reports, and other writings about the ugly events of April 26, 1915. Many of these are cited in this writing. Despite all of this work and assistance, I'm sure that there are still a few problems with the story and its details, not uncommon for researching an event from more than a century ago.

To everyone who has assisted with this project, thanks for helping to introduce me to my family's history.

Floy Maye Fryer, the author's Aunt Toots, was a key element in the shootings and the following legal cases. For years, she was also the family spokesperson whenever the subject of the murders came up. This photo is of Maye during the 1920s after she had married Clay Chester Sisemore. Photo from the collection of Tomme Jennings.

Introduction

In a wholesale murder at Solgahachia [sic], 10 miles north of Morrilton, about 8 o'clock tonight, Sam Bell, a young cattle buyer, killed his father-in-law, Dick Fryer; his brother-in-law, Amos Fryer; his sister-in-law, Mrs. Earl Bearden; and her husband.

Daily Arkansas Gazette
Page 1 – April 27, 1915

This quote from a newspaper article begins the story. In many ways, it was like the gunfights of the old west – shots were fired back and forth between combatants. In this case, it involves a gunman with a history of violence shooting down innocent homesteaders. It also reminds many of the current issues with crime; some people commit crime after crime but are never stopped by the law until they commit murder, and even then, they seem to be the victims and receive most of the support and attention. However you look at the murders of April 26, 1915, it was a terrible tragedy that never should have happened.

How serious the shootings were to the community, and even the State of Arkansas, was shown by their ability to push articles about statewide flooding and the war in Europe off of the front pages of many newspapers. These news reports didn't end in a few days, but continued through the months of trials, and spanned years due to the escape and recapture of Bell, and his later furlough. For example, a review of the *Arkansas Gazette* found more than two dozen articles about the killings, funerals, and trials on pages 1 and 2 over just two months in 1915. The story wasn't just carried locally, but was reported upon in newspapers from coast to coast and border to border. Papers such as the *New York Times*, *Boston Evening Globe*, *Evening Star* (Washington, D.C.), *Newark Evening Star* (Newark, New Jersey), *The Barre Daily Times* (Barre, Vermont), *Manchester Democrat* (Manchester, Iowa), *The Montgomery Advertiser* (Montgomery, Alabama), *Dakota Farmers' Leader* (Canton, South Dakota), *Iron County News* (Hurley, Wisconsin), *The Log Cabin Democrat* (Conway, Arkansas), and others all reported on the murders due to the drama, and the later legal significance that the trials acquired.

Nothing makes a person appreciate their existence more than looking back at a family history. Disease, war, the dangers of crossing a river, a hungry mountain lion or bear, or even a stray bullet, could mean that I wouldn't exist. For the Fryer Family, the actions on April 26, 1915, ended the lives of many family members, and impacted those of others for the rest of their lives. For me, if my grandmother hadn't been at her brother's home, and later hid in a neighbor's house during that night, I might not be writing this today. Her and her family's attempt to forget the shootings also made it very difficult to determine many of the facts of the story. What is included here comes from family legend, court records, and the reporting of many newspapers. It was a challenge to assemble.

This book, or any book, will never be able to tell the full story. All who were there are long dead. Therefore, it is the goal of this volume to tell the basic story of the Fryer family at Solgohachia, the story of the murders, and what happened to the survivors after that frightful night. Additional information is always welcomed.

The Fryer family arrived in North America from England during the earliest days of settlement, and farmed in the Carolina area before working west through Tennessee,

Introduction

Alabama and then to Arkansas. Some members of the family made it as far west as California. This story focuses on those who came to what became Solgohachia, Arkansas, where the tragedy of April 26, 1915, took place.

The event on Monday, April 26, 1915, has been described as the "most terrible thing to happen at Solgohachia," and possibly in all of Conway County. In this case, a feud between a former in-law and the Fryer family (and many other members of the Solgohachia community) resulted in four deaths and a series of legal rulings that still impact Arkansas and national law. While there are some conflicts in the stories told by different involved parties, every effort has been made to document the facts. However, many of the details have been forgotten as the Fryer family attempted to forget the murders, family members moved away or died, and finally the farm was sold off. Most of those who were there never talked about the murders, and only the reports in newspapers across the country and a few family stories remain. This book is an attempt to tell the story using all of the sources possible so that those who died are never forgotten.

There is one major caution to the reader – the names can often be confusing. The Fryer family had a strong tradition that nicknames were used for pretty much everyone, often names that had nothing to do with the member's real name. Family members also often had their names spelled multiple ways, which can cause further confusion. This is especially true for one of the main parties in the story – Barbara Abigail Fryer. Her name was often spelled Barbra, but she was called Abby, often spelled Abbie, even in the various court records. Additionally, many of the women used names based upon old English tradition – you would take a man's name and add the "e" sound to the end. Thus, names like Jerry, Johny, Billie, Willie, and Tomme will be found and used by both men and women.

The same issue of having multiple names applied to Earl Bearden, the husband of Abbie Fryer. While his name was Earl, it was never used. Instead, Erdie was the informal name, Eard the formal name, and Erd the simplified name. Erdie will be used since that is what is on his gravestone.

Because of the confusion these different names and spellings can cause, the various versions of each person's name will be pointed out but only one name will be used throughout this book.

The Fryer Family Prior to 1915

Various parts of the Fryer family left England and began arriving in what became the United States by the early 1600s, with settlers in Virginia (the year 1623) and Massachusetts (a bit more than a decade later in 1639) leading the way. By the mid-1600s, several branches of the Fryer family had arrived in Virginia, and they had spread out to Maryland and the Carolinas (North and South Carolina were one large colony until 1729).

Besides the spelling as Fryer, the name was also recorded as being Freer and Frier during this time, and actually swapped back and forth from time to time. Tracking these various branches can be very confusing as all seemed to use the first names of Edward, George, John, Thomas, and William, and they seemed to have moved often. This was not that unusual at the time as farms could seldom be divided between the many children, so parts of the family often moved west and south to newly available lands.

There was also the tradition of naming children after the father and mother, and their close relations. This means that there are many names that have been used generation after generation. Some names were even used for multiple children within the same family, sometimes after the death of the first child or with different middle names and nicknames. Without knowing the exact birth and death dates, this can cause a great deal of error within the family history. Various histories of the different Fryer family branches often conflict, and the information used here is as accurate as possible.

The Fryer Movement West

Many of the first settlers in early Arkansas traced their history to the Atlantic Seaboard. They generally moved westward after the American Revolution, and then southward as land became available due to the movement of the Native Tribes towards Indian Territory, and the sale of homestead land by the federal government. As families grew, many moved further west to Arkansas, with some moving on to places like Oklahoma and California. The same pattern applied to the Fryer Family.

Out of these many early Fryers came George Fryer, who lived in what became South Carolina during the mid to late 1700s. The date of his birth and much of his history are unknown, but it is known that he married a woman named Mary Ann. Among their children was John Fryer, a successful farmer near Barnwell, South Carolina.

John Fryer (1753-1805) was born in Barnwell, in the South Carolina Colony, on June 1, 1753. His parents were George (unknown-1796) and Mary Ann Fryer (1730-unknown). The South Carolina Colony was once part of the larger Carolina Colony, which was split into North Carolina and South Carolina in 1729 when both became royal colonies protected by the English crown. Farming and trade dominated the region at the time. In 1773, John married Sarah Bush, who was born in Bertie, North Carolina, in 1755. Her parents were Isaac Bush (1727-1795) and Catharine Franck Bush (1724-1788).

John Fryer was my great-great-great-great-great-grandfather, and seemed to be involved with both farming and several businesses. He reportedly operated a small store, consolidated crops of area farmers for sale to regional markets, and apparently sometimes hauled freight with his wagon. John and Sarah were the parents of at least two sons, one of whom was John William Fryer (1775-1820). The couple remained at Barnwell until their deaths - John on June 1, 1805, and Sarah in 1811. However, their son, John William Fryer, began the family move westward.

John William Fryer (1775-1820) was the son of John (1753-1805) and Sarah Bush Fryer (1755-1811). Some histories give his birth date as February 13th and his birth place as North Carolina. John William Fryer was my great-great-great-great-grandfather. John William was apparently a wanderer, as he married Rachel Holland (1775-?) in East Tennessee in 1797. This was probably a typical frontier relationship where an informal marriage initially took place, and then a formal marriage happened when the proper authorities were available. Rachel Holland was the daughter of Abraham Holland (1715-1800) and Asenath Spiers (1730-1802), who were married about 1752 in Maryland. Asenath was the second wife of Abraham Holland, who had married Nancy Simpson in 1735. Some records show that the Holland family had 14 children, and two were named Rachel.

There is a great deal of confusion about John William Fryer and Rachel Holland. There was apparently a John Fryer who was born in Maryland who later moved to South Carolina, and a number of area histories seem to mix up their stories. What is known is that John and Rachel Fryer had one son, William "Dick" Fryer, who was born in Tennessee on September 4, 1796, a year before their formal marriage.

During the early 1800s, land in Alabama became available as homesteads. This was especially true when large amounts of land becoming available about 1815 after the Creek Indians ceded much of their lands, creating "Alabama Fever." About this time, John William's family moved to farmland in what became Bibb County, Alabama. Here,

John William Fryer died. There is no clear record of his burial, or what happened to Rachel.

William "Dick" Fryer (1796-1865) was the Fryer family leader who moved his family from Alabama to Arkansas. He is also my great-great-great-grandfather. Dick was born in Tennessee on September 4, 1796, to John William Fryer (1775-1820) and Rachel Holland (1775-?). He married Nancy Chamberlain Sersey (1798-1840) on October 29, 1815, in Bibb County, Alabama. The two had 14 children - Henry (1816-1817), John (1817-1850s), Pleasant (1819-1823), Richard Chamberlain (1821-1888), Henry (1822-?), James (1825-1844), Sarah Ann (1826-?), Elizabeth (1828-?), Jeremiah (1830-1872), Nancy C. (1832-?), William (1833-1834), Mary Ann (1834-?), Tabitha (1836-1922), and Francis T. (1837-1852).

Little is known of the early years of **Nancy Chamberlain Sersey** except that she was born in Tennessee on March 4, 1798, and her father's name was reportedly Henry Sersey. There is actually some conflict about Nancy's name as the death certificate of her daughter Tabitha states that it was Mary. Nancy Fryer died on July 12, 1840, at Bibb County, Alabama. A few years later (1843), Dick Fryer married Lydia J. Hicks, who had been born in Kentucky about 1802. Almost immediately, the family moved from Bibb County, located in the central portion of Alabama, southwest of today's Birmingham, to what was shown as Pleasant Hill, in Conway County, Arkansas.

In the 1860 census, William Fryer was shown to live in Washington Township of Conway County. Mail service was shown to be provided from Lewisburg. The farm at the time was valued at $3000. Living with William were two grandsons, Francis and William, the children of John Fryer, who had passed away a few years earlier. There were also two men who had been hired to work on the farm. William

"Dick" Fryer passed away in Conway County, Arkansas, on August 25, 1865, outliving at least one of his wives and many of his children. There is no record of where his burial took place. The Fryer Cemetery was active at the time, but few records exist of its use.

Some of the children of Dick and Nancy died young (Henry, Pleasant and William), while others scattered across the country (Richard, Nancy and Tabitha). At least one remained in Alabama (second Henry), and others moved to Arkansas, helping to create a community alongside Point Remove Creek that was known as Fryer.

Richard Chamberlain Fryer (1821-1888) married Caroline Veazey in Bibb County, Alabama, on October 15, 1839. They moved to Arkansas with the rest of the family, and then on to California during the early 1850s. There, records show that he was a minister and farmer, and during 1870, a church was organized in the family home. The church later became the Pomona First Baptist Church. When he died on December 8, 1888, Richard was buried in the Spadra Cemetery at Pomona, California.

Richard Chamberlain Fryer was the father of Jeremiah L. Fryer (1849-1902), an investor and developer in California and Arizona. Jere or Jerry is probably most famous as marrying Pauline Cushman (1833-1893) in 1879, one of the most famous Union spies during the Civil War. Several books cover the story of Pauline and her husband.

Nancy C. Fryer (1832-?) married Benjamin Holyfield in 1850 after moving to Arkansas with her parents. Benjamin and Nancy joined the wagon train of Captain Johnson, along with Richard C. Fryer, heading to California in November of 1852. A number of Conway County residents were part of the wagon train, including the parents of Benjamin Holyfield. Nancy disappeared by the 1860 census.

Tabitha (1836-1922) also moved with her family to Arkansas, where she married Nathan M. McCaige in 1852.

After the Civil War, the family reportedly took a train west to California, where they eventually settled on a farm near Tehachapi. Nathan died in 1880, and Tabitha married James Flannigan from Ireland, who had been a boarder at her home. In 1884, she married again, this time to Edward Hicklin from Pomona. They were divorced in the 1890s. Tabitha passed away in Highland Park, California, on February 18, 1922.

There is little information about Sarah Ann Fryer, who was born on May 4, 1826. Henry Fryer (1822-?), who was named to replace the Henry Fryer who died at age 4 months, married Melissa Alelene (?) in Alabama. He died while in Dallas County, Alabama, and his wife joined the family in Arkansas and remarried on May 6, 1860. The rest of the children of Dick and Nancy traveled with them to Arkansas. John Fryer (1817-?) was born on November 21, 1817, in Selma, Alabama. He married Sarah Cassandra and moved with the family to Conway County, Arkansas, where he died. James Fryer (1825–1844) was born in Selma, Dallas County, Alabama, on January 14, 1825, and died on February 4, 1844, at Pleasant Hill, Conway County, Arkansas.

The history of two daughters is confusing. Elizabeth Fryer (1828-?) was born in Bibb County, Alabama, on January 13, 1828. She married Benjamin T. Crow on April 15, 1846. No records exist of Elizabeth after 1870, and her youngest children were living with her older daughter in 1880. Mary Ann Fryer (1834-?) was born on October 7, 1834, in Centreville, the county seat of Bibb County, Alabama. She married a Thomas Anthony in 1850 in Conway County, apparently soon divorced him and married Anthony Lucas by 1852. They had several children through the early 1870s, when records about Mary Ann Fryer Lucas end. A third daughter, Francis T. Fryer (1837-1852) was born in Centreville, Alabama (November 27, 1837), and died (April 21,

1852) in Pleasant Hill, Arkansas, located in Conway County.

It should be noted that as the Fryer family moved to Conway County in Arkansas, some confusion in the records do exist. The spelling of the family name sometimes was changed, or at least it was misspelled. For example, the 1850 and 1860 Federal census for Conway County showed people with the names Fryer, Fryar, Friar and Frier. However, Fryer was the common spelling used by this branch of the family.

Jeremiah "Jerry" Fryer (1830-1872) is part of the direct line to the 1915 tragedy at Solgohachia, and was my great-great-grandfather. He was part of the Fryer family from Alabama that moved to Conway County, Arkansas, during the early 1840s. Jerry was born in Bibb County, Alabama, on November 27, 1830, the ninth child of eleven. His parents were William (1796-1865) and Nancy Sersey Fryer (1798-1840).

In 1856, he married **Nancy Jane Minyard**, who was born in Arkansas on October 12, 1832. They lived near the rest of the Fryer family in one of a number of houses on the various Fryer farms. The 1860 census reported that Jerry Fryer was a farmer with an estate value of $700. Living in the same household was his wife Nancy, a 1-year-old named Sarah, and Thomas Brown, hired to work on the farm. The Sarah was likely Sarah Elizabeth Fryer Oliver, known later as Aunt Sarah. She lived by herself much of her life in a small house on the James P. Fryer farm because she had tuberculosis. She passed away on March 20, 1934. Jerry Fryer passed away near what became Solgohachia on June 9, 1872. He was buried in the Fryer Cemetery on the family farm. His wife Nancy continued to live with the Fryers and passed away on March 13, 1902, and was also buried in the Fryer Cemetery.

Jerry and Nancy had three sons. The first was Richard T. Fryer (1860–1915), who has direct connections to the 1915 tragedy at Solgohachia and who's story will be told later. The second son was James P. Fryer (1863-1934), who was born on January 5, 1863. There is no clear record of where James was born, likely because Union forces were in the area at the time and many families moved about to avoid their presence. James married Mollie Holder (1869-1919), and they had five children – Annie (1895-1949), Ollie (1897-1969), Nettie Faye (1900-1959), Ruby (1904-1979) and James (1908-1908). James P. Fryer and his family lived on a farm near Hattieville, a few miles west of the farm of Richard T. Fryer. Mollie Holder Fryer died on January 26, 1919, and James P. Fryer died on September 12, 1934. All are buried in the Solgohachia Friendship Community Cemetery.

James P. Fryer worked the farm of Dick Fryer after Dick's murder in 1915. Like many members of the Fryer family, James P. was buried in the Solgohachia Friendship Community Cemetery. Photo by Barton Jennings.

The third son was William Henry Fryer (1870-1904). William was born on September 17, 1870, and married Mary Ellen Barnes during the 1890s. Mary Ellen was younger, having been born on November 28, 1879. Their first child was Jerry David Fryer (1899-1982), who died in Ashley County, Arkansas, and was buried in the Oak Grove Cemetery in West Carroll Parish, Louisiana. Their second child was a daughter, Ella (1901-1981). She is buried in the Adams Cemetery near Solgohachia. Richard Layfatte Fryer (1903-1989) was the last son, and he is buried in the Solgohachia Friendship Community Cemetery. William Henry Fryer died during September 1904, and was buried in the Fryer Cemetery at Solgohachia. Mary Ellen remarried, becoming the wife of Robert Harlow Poteet. She died on February 11, 1950, and is buried in the Solgohachia Friendship Community Cemetery.

The Fryer Family in Arkansas

The Fryer Family was one of a number of families that moved to western Arkansas in the 1830s and 1840s. The first settlers in the area were trappers and traders, and some who were fugitives from the law. They generally settled on the rich and fertile lands along the Arkansas River. From 1817 to 1828, the Western Cherokee occupied a reservation in Arkansas that included this part of the Territory. In 1828, the Cherokee gave up this land in return for a new reservation in what became known as Indian Territory, today's Oklahoma. With this movement, cheap and fertile land became available in the Arkansas Valley region of western Arkansas. Additionally, with the construction of the Little Rock & Fort Smith Railway, lands were granted to the railroad to sell to pay for the line's construction. Sales of these lands began before the Civil War and continued until the early 1900s.

For decades, some of the Fryer family members were involved with the local county government and later the post office at Solgohachia. For example, county records for November 1850 reported that John H. Fryer was one of the Commissioners appointed to locate the "seat of Justice for Conway County." At the same time, Richard Chamberlain Fryer was holding the title of Justice of Peace for Conway County. An interesting note from November 6, 1850, was that the county owed Richard Fryer a "sum of six dollars and twelve and a half cents for fees due him in certain State cases." The same day, John Fryer filed a claim "for the sum of twenty-five dollars for services rendered as Commissioner to locate the seat of Justice for Conway County."

By the late 1800s and early 1900s, the Fryer family was well-established in Conway County, with a number of branches of the family living on area farms. The numbers were so great that maps showed the community of Fryer, located just a few miles west of Solgohachia, Arkansas.

The Community of Solgohachia

The site of the Fryer Family murders was west of the small community of Solgohachia, Arkansas. Solgohachia (pronounced "saw-guh-HATCH-ee", or simply "saw-guh" or "saw-go") is one of hundreds of small rural Arkansas communities that are still scattered across the state. The town was large enough to have a post office by the late 1870s, but it was never more than the home of a few stores and several hundred residents.

Solgohachia was located about ten miles north of Lewisburg, a port town founded in 1825 on the Arkansas River. Solgohachia was at a strategic location, the gap between Jenkins Mountain, Ragsdale Mountain, and Tucker Mountain. This gap was at the first major ridge north of Lewisburg, meaning that any river trade with communities to the north had to pass through Solgohachia.

During much of the 1800s, Lewisburg was an important port town, so being on the route northward into the farmlands and hills also made Solgohachia important. Lewisburg (originally Lewisburgh) started about 1820 when Major William Lewis, his son, Stephen D. Lewis, and Dr. Nimrod P. Menifee established a port settlement where Point Remove Creek flowed into the Arkansas River. A trading post known as Lewisburgh was opened by Stephen D. Lewis in 1825. The combination of a river port and a trading post made Lewisburgh one of the most important locations in Western Arkansas.

Conway County was created as Arkansas' 11th county on October 20, 1825. Using lands that were once part of Pulaski County, the new county was named for Henry Wharton Conway, Arkansas' territorial delegate to the U.S.

Congress. The county originally covered about 2500 square miles, but gave up much of its land to the newer counties of Faulkner, Perry, Pope, Van Buren, and Yell. Today, the county includes 640 square miles.

When the county was created, the town of Cadron became the temporary county seat. In 1829, the county seat moved to the home of Stephen Harris (Harrisburg) until a more permanent location could be chosen. In 1831, property was acquired from Dr. Menifee to be the location of a courthouse and jail for Conway County. Dr. Nimrod Menifee and Stephen D. Lewis built a log cabin courthouse and the county seat moved to Lewisburgh that year. The following year, a post office opened and kept using the name Lewisburgh, even when the community shortened its name to Lewisburg.

By the early 1850s, Lewisburg was a thriving river town, but its location at the south end of the county created problems for many residents. Because of this, the county seat moved again in 1850 when Springfield obtained the title. In 1871, the Little Rock & Fort Smith Railroad was building west toward Fort Smith. This construction could place Lewisburg on both the Arkansas River and a railroad, and after donating $5000 for a new courthouse and $10,000 for a stone jail, Lewisburg was again the county seat starting in 1873.

Unfortunately for Lewisburg, the railroad was built about a mile to the north, and a new town was platted on the property of Edwin James Morrill, George H. Morrill, and James Miles Moose. Reportedly a flip of a coin made the town Morrilton instead of Mooseville. However, Moose Street was located just east of the railroad's station. Morrilton quickly grew with 770 residents in 1880 and 1644 in 1890. Meanwhile, Lewisburg saw its population drop from a reported 2000 in 1860 to 356 in 1880. The Lewisburgh post office closed in 1882, and the county seat moved to

Morrilton in 1883. Within a few years, Lewisburg was little more than a ferry landing with just a few residents, many occupying the abandoned homes made available when other residents moved northward.

Point Remove

Point Remove played an important role in the development of Solgohachia, Lewisburg, and much of Conway County. However, the name is greatly misunderstood. Point Remove dates back to the French exploration of the area and was used for the location where Point Remove Creek flows into the Arkansas River. This created a whirlpool or eddy, a remous in French. In an 1813 document, William Lovely used the term "point remove byo," or Point Remove Bayou, for the creek. Thomas Nuttall, a naturalist who explored much of the region and wrote the book *Journal of Travels into the Arkansas Territory during the year 1819*, called the area Point Remu. During 1819-1820, Major Stephen Long led an expedition that passed along the Arkansas River. His report called the location Point Remove, or Eddy Point Creek.

Point Remove took on major significance when it became the southern point of the boundary line for the Treaty of the Cherokee Agency of 1817. This treaty established a line from "Budwells Old Place" at the mouth of Point Remove Creek, to the White River at Shields Ferry near Batesville, Arkansas. Lands to the west were traded to the Cherokees in return for lands east of the Mississippi River, and it temporarily became the western border of the Arkansas Territory. The agreement of 1828 that moved the border further west called Point Remove "Pointe au Remou." This use of the term led some to mistakenly believe that is was named for the removal of the Cherokees from what became Arkansas to Indian Territory in today's

Oklahoma. For those who are interested, the Old Cherokee Boundary Line, also sometimes known as the Old Indian Treaty Boundary, still shows on many maps and is often used on land descriptions and surveys in Arkansas.

During the early 1820s, Lewisburg developed east of Point Remove, but a post office also opened nearby in 1824 using the name Point Remove. The Point Remove post office opened and closed several times in slightly different locations, slowly moving northward up Point Remove Creek. By 1870, the Point Remove post office was located in the home of Dr. Francis Marion Crowell, Sr. At the time, Crowell's house was located on the Fryer farm, near "Friar's Ford" on the East Fork of the Point Remove Creek. Reports state that Dr. Crowell moved closer to what became Solgohachia in 1873, still operating the Point Remove post office.

The Town of Solgohachia

The slopes between Jenkins Mountain and Ragsdale Mountain had been the site of a small settlement since the early 1800s. Initially, the Osage Tribe controlled this area. From 1817 to 1828, the land was part of the Arkansas reservation of the Western Cherokee. With the removal of the Cherokee to Indian Territory, the land north and west of Lewisburg opened to American settlement. The gap was on a natural trade route between the farms in the Ozark Mountains to the north, and the Arkansas River to the south. However, the town that formed was never legally organized, and it wasn't until 1876 that a post office was located in the community.

The start of what became Solgohachia is generally traced to William Smith, who homesteaded 80 acres there about 1870. Smith promoted the area, and a Mr. Clopton opened a blacksmith shop nearby. Little is known about Clopton, but seven members of the Clopton family are buried in the

Old Antioch Cemetery in nearby Morrilton. A number of other families soon built houses in the community, and stores were opened by the Willis and McClure families. Louis M. McClure and other members of the family were buried in the Solgohachia Friendship Cemetery during the 1870s and 1880s.

About the same time, the Point Remove post office was located west of town along the East Fork of Point Remove Creek. Maps from the time showed Point Remove as being near today's Wesley Chapel along Arkansas Highway 95. The post office for a number of years was at the home of Dr. Francis Marion Crowell, Sr., located on the Fryer Farm. In 1873, Dr. Crowell moved to a farm closer to Solgohachia, but kept the Point Remove name for his post office. His move east continued in 1876 when McClure sold his store to Crowell. This move created problems as a new application for the post office was required, and complications came about as there were now a number of postal facilities that included the word point. This required the selection of a new name for Crowell's post office, and likely the community itself.

While several names were reportedly considered, Solgohachia was chosen and approved for the post office by 1878. Local histories state that the name came from Dr. Crowell, although a number of various stories exist about the name. Reportedly, Crowell had once lived near Solgohachee Creek in Alabama, and found the name to be unique. For some reason, the Post Office Department changed the spelling to Solgohachie, and then to Solgohachia as the paperwork was completed. Another name also came up in the area as a new post office named Arthur opened about 1880 to serve farmers along the lower part of Point Remove. This post office closed in 1915, with rural routes from the Solgohachia post office handling the business. The Saint Vincent post office, located to the northwest, closed in 1918 and its routes and services were also taken over by Solgohachia,

The Solgohachia post office had a number of postmasters over the years, generally from some of the leading families of the community. By 1881, the postmaster was Reverend Berryman Hicks Bearden, then during April 1884, William F. Nabours acquired the title. A few years later, George B. Bearden was the postmaster, but when he moved west, William L. Presley became the postmaster of Solgohachia. By 1894, the postmaster was Hiram Campbell Gordon, with his daughter Arkansas "Arka" Gordon handling the job by 1897. Soon, the Fryer family assumed the title of postmaster, with Richard T. Fryer, Abbie Fryer, and then Maye Fryer all holding the job.

Solgohachia grew quickly, and during the early 1880s was considered as the location of a new county seat. Four communities vied for the prize - Morrilton, Plumerville, Solgohachia, and Springfield. After the first vote, there was no clear winner, so a second vote was held between Morrilton and Solgohachia. Morrilton, the larger community, won the vote and became the county seat in 1883.

Little has actually been published about Solgohachia, and one of the most in-depth historical articles is found in what is known as *Goodspeed's History*, or more precisely the *Biographical and Historical Memoirs of Western Arkansas*, published by Goodspeed Publishers in 1891. A description of Solgohachia can be found in the chapter on Conway County. Its states that "Solgohachia is a thrifty and growing village in Washington Township, nine miles north of Morrilton. The leading spirit in its development has been Mr. M. Crowell, who started the first store there about eleven years ago. It now has three general stores conducted by M. Crowell, A. B. Simmons and W. F. Kirkland; one drug store by Walsh & Presley; Walker & Nabors, blacksmiths and woodworkers. Three physicians – W. L. Presley, W. T. Morrow and Z. T. Kindred. W. L. Presley, Postmaster." The book also states that the "Conway County landscape is rolling farmlands, forested ridges, isolated mountains and lakes. The county lies in the Ozark foothills."

Crowell's name seemed to have popped up a number of times during the 1800s. Dr. Francis Marion Crowell, Sr., was born in North Carolina, moved to Alabama, and then to Conway County, Arkansas. He was a trained physician who also operated a series of post offices and a general store. Dr. Crowell and his sons were in the mercantile business at Solgohachia until about 1907. Members of his family are buried in nearby Center Ridge and Morrilton, as well as in the Crowell Cemetery southwest of Solgohachia.

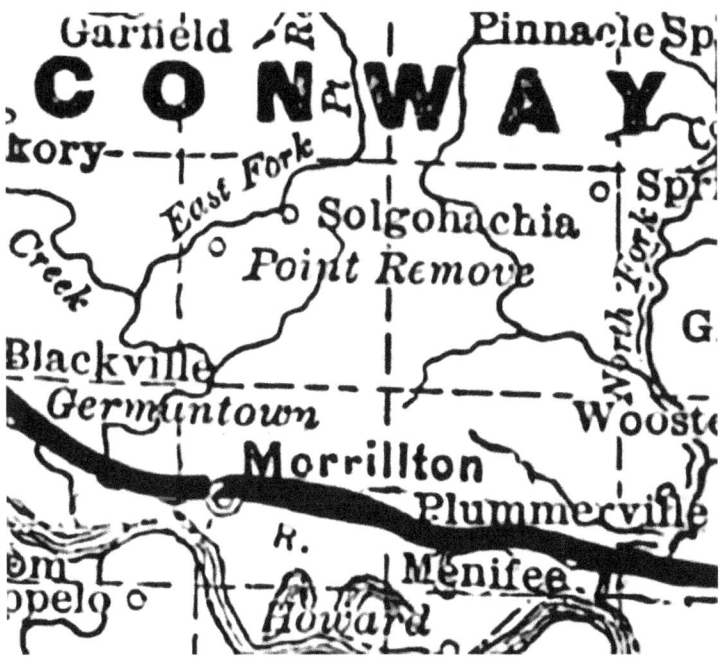

This *Cram's township and rail road map of Arkansas* from 1895 shows Conway County and the location of Solgohachia. Cram, George Franklin, 1841-1928. Chicago, 1895. Library of Congress, Geography and Map Division. https://www.loc.gov/resource/g4001p.rr001840/?r=0.3 61%2C0.245%2C0.179%2C0.072%2C0&st=image

The Name Solgohachia

There is a great deal of conflict in where the name Solgohachia came from. One version of the naming states that Dr. M. Crowell, an early settler who controlled a local post office, chose Solgohachee because there was a Solgohachee Creek where he once lived in Alabama. Records indicate that there was a Creek village using a version of the name Solgohachee in Alabama in 1760. Some of the first European settlers called a creek near the Alabama village "Rattle Creek." This came from the Creek terms sougo (cymbal) and hatche (creek), according to the works of Henry Rowe Schoolcraft (*Information Respecting the History, Condition and Prospects of the Indian Tribes of the United States: Collected and Prepared Under the Direction of the Bureau of Indian Affairs per Act of Congress of March 3rd, 1847 – Part IV*). Reportedly the Post Office Department changed the Arkansas name to Solgohachie, and even later they changed it again to Solgohachia.

A second version of the naming says that it came from the Choctaw word Sok-ko-huch-cha, meaning "muscadine river." The muscadine is a native type of grapevine that grows from the southeast across the country to eastern Texas and Oklahoma. Native tribes, and later white settlers, cultivated the vines and used the berries for juice, jellies and wines.

A third version of the naming states that Solgohachia means "a hole in the mountain" and refers to the pass between the various mountains in the area. This name seems appropriate because of the location of the community, a gap in the first major ridge north of the Arkansas River, surrounded by Jenkins, Ragsdale, and Tucker mountains.

The fourth version of the name is certainly the most romantic. It states that the Indian Chief Ponti established his capital just west of the Old Cherokee Boundary Line,

The Community of Solgohachia

on the high hill (Jenkins Mountain) to the west of today's Solgohachia. Supposedly, around his camp, a number of other settlements quickly developed, created by others who had reached here on the Trail of Tears. Reportedly, a great warrior named Sol eventually won the affection of the beautiful daughter, Gowafa, of Chief Ponti. Their wedding took place under an oak next to a well which never ran dry. From the names of Sol and Gowafa came the name Solgohachia. The area is rich in artifacts, and Indians and settlers often dug in the hills looking for any buried treasure left by Chief Ponti.

The possible Indian heritage of the Solgohachia name is promoted by this sign for the Solgohachia Park. Photo by Barton Jennings.

This version of the town's naming is so popular that for many years a marker erected by the Morrilton High School Beta Club stood in front of Richard W. Ruff's grocery store and the old Solgohachia post office, next to an old well.

This marker read "Solgohachia. M.H.S. Beta Club, 1962-1963. Years ago in this square Chief Ponti's beautiful daughter Gowafa married the favorite warrior Sol. Today some still believe the well insures each new bride lasting beauty and happiness through its waters."

The Morrilton High School Beta Club marker no longer stands at Solgohachia due to a recent highway realignment. However, it was found leaning against a small building during 2023. Photo by Barton Jennings.

Today's Solgohachia

The late 1800s and early 1900s were the peak of business at Solgohachia. While the Crowell family stayed in the mercantile business until the early 1900s, new leadership at the Sologohachia post office was needed by the late 1880s. The Bearden family farmed in the area, and George B. Bearden was the postmaster at Sologohachia in July 1887. Starting in 1888, the postmaster was William L. Presley, a physician and partner in the Walsh & Presley drug and grocery store in town. By 1895, Arkansas "Arka" Gordon (daughter of Sarah Angeline Bearden Gordon and Hiram Campbell Gordon) was the postmaster. At the time, the Solgohachia post office was authorized to issue and pay money-orders, making it an important station in Conway County. In 1903, Mrs. Louisa R. Truce was shown as the postal clerk at Solgohachia. By 1909, Barbara A. Fryer was serving as postmaster, with her father Richard T. Fryer acting as clerk. In 1911, records show that Mrs. Barbara A. Bearden (now her married name) was postmaster with a compensation of $130. Various members of the Fryer family were involved with the local post office for years.

Starting on June 25, 1935, Civilian Conservation Corps Company 3789 located near Sologohachia. Much of the Company was made up of members of units being closed, and it located at Sologohachia as a soil conservation unit. The newspaper of Company 3789 reported on the arrival of the unit. "After driving from Morrilton to Birdtown in search of the camp site, a recheck was made and this time the newly built camp was located near Solgohachia in Mr. Scroggin's persimmon patch." The location of the camp was later described as "the government's five-acre tract of land located nine miles northwest of Morrilton and within gunshot of the Indian village of Solgohachia." At its peak, Company 3789 had more than one hundred area farms under cooperative agreements where they were working to improve soil conditions, end erosion, and increase crop yields.

The businesses slowly moved away or closed as Morrilton grew. Paved roads made Solgohachia easier to access, and many workers started to commute from here. Today, the unincorporated community is still located at the junction of Arkansas Highways 9 and 287, less than ten miles north of Interstate 40 at Morrilton. The community features a post office, the Solgohachia Baptist Church, a few abandoned stores, and a number of houses. The Solgohachia Friendship Community Cemetery can be found behind the post office on Arkansas Highway 9.

A relatively recent change in the Solgohachia area has been the development of the natural gas industry. Hundreds of wells are now nearby, providing unexpected wealth for a number of local farmers and landowners. Additionally, the poultry industry exists west of town, and several campgrounds and religious retreats are located in the surrounding hills. Ranching and hay production can also be found, and the area features about 500 residents. With all of the changes, for the most part, the surrounding hills are again green with forests.

While Solgohachia is today little more than a post office, cemetery, and a road junction surrounded by houses, signs along the various highways still mark its name. Photo by Barton Jennings.

Fryer's Ford Bridge

Passing north and west of Solgohachia is East Fork Point Remove Creek. The stream forms on the southwest side of Hunter Mountain near Formosa in southern Van Buren County. It flows generally to the southwest and merges with the West Fork northeast of Blackwell. These two streams separate the north end of Conway County from the south end. The combined waters then flow southward, passing west of Morrilton before flowing into the Arkansas River at Point Remove. The *Biographical and Historical Memoirs of Western Arkansas* (Goodspeed Publishers, 1891) described the stream by stating it "flows, in general, in a southern direction, but with a very winding course, and empties into the Arkansas 1½ miles above the City of Morrilton. Although there is much land under cultivation along the valley of this beautiful stream, there are thousands of acres yet a waiting occupation." Some sources state that locals called the stream "Pointymove," a shortened version of Point Remove.

While a number of versions of the stream's name have been used, today the Arkansas Department of Transportation calls it the East Fork Point Remove Creek, according to this sign along Arkansas Highway 95 west of Fryer's Ford. Photo by Barton Jennings.

The Solgohachia Murders

In 1856, the road to Fryer's Ford was the subject of a Conway County Court ruling. At the time, it was declared to be a part of a local road district.

> *Now on this day it is ordered by the Court that the road commencing at Lewisburg and running to Glass Village from the Welborn township line to the ford of Point Remove Creek near William Fryer's be and the same is hereby designated as Road District No. One (1) of Washington township and it is further ordered by the Court that Joseph Gordon be and he is hereby appointed Overseer of said road and that the late Overseer (Wm. D. McCaig) is hereby ordered to deliver to the said Joseph Gordon the apportionment of hands heretofore apportioned to him by Henry Fryer Esqr. and that said Joseph L. Gordon is hereby authorized to proceed with said hands to keep up said road according to law.*

Much of the Fryer family lived alongside the stream three miles west of Solgohachia, and the local ford became known as Fryer's Ford, sometimes spelled Friar's Ford. With it being the only crossing of the stream for many miles, the ford and local road were somewhat busy. However, the Solgohachia postmaster noted in 1878 that Point Remove Creek was "bad to cross." All along the creek, various churches held baptism celebrations in the stream. The area around Fryer's Ford was one of these locations, and numerous reports about all-day religious celebrations were recorded for decades.

Fryer's Ford Bridge

Baptism celebrations at Fryer's Ford were a fairly common event, and this photo shows the size that some of these events obtained. Photo from the collection of Tomme Jennings.

During the 1880s, Conway County began building bridges along many of the important roads. However, it wasn't until 1889 that the county leaders appointed a committee to examine sites "at or near Fryer's Ford for the purpose of building a new bridge." The original plans were to build a wooden bridge, but the locations around Fryer's Ford were too wide, so planning changed to building an iron bridge.

A challenge in locating and building the bridge was the channel of East Fork Point Remove Creek, created by almost yearly floods as the stream forced its way between Jenkins Mountain to southeast, and Pigeon Roost Mountain to northwest. The creek had created its own small valley as it changed channels based upon the water levels. Even at the best locations, the stream was more than 100 feet wide and would require the stabilization of the banks.

A location was finally chosen a short distance downstream from the site of Fryer's Ford.

By the end of 1889, announcements were made about the bridge, and in January 1890, the Conway County Court awarded a series of contracts for what became known as the Fryer's Ford Bridge. Construction of the stone abutments was assigned to local stone mason Alfred Cook, while a $3898 contract for the iron superstructure was awarded to the Wrought Iron Bridge Company of Canton, Ohio.

The bridge was not cheaply built by a no-name manufacturer. The Wrought Iron Bridge Company was incorporated in 1871 by David Hammond, W.R. Reeves and Jon Abbott. The firm was created to take over an older Canton foundry, and to manufacture and market their patented iron truss bridges. By 1881, the firm had built bridges in twenty-five states. The firm was known for its Pratt through truss spans that had been "almost universally adopted for both railway and highway bridges of moderate span." The company was so successful that in April 1900, it became part of the American Bridge Company, and was fully merged into the new company in 1901. As the firm's history states: "American Bridge Company was formed as a JP Morgan & Company engineered merger of 28 steel companies in 1900." The new bridge firm was created as a subsidiary of United States Steel, giving it both an engineering and construction advantage, but also a steel supply advantage. The new company immediately dominated the market.

The Pratt through truss design was patented by Caleb and Thomas Pratt in 1844. Caleb and Thomas Pratt were a father-and-son team from Boston, with Caleb an architect and Thomas an engineer. The design was very popular through the early twentieth century, and first was made up of a combination wood and iron truss. Later it was made of iron and then steel, one of the few designs that was successful with all three types of building materials. The design passed its forces throughout the structure, with the diagonal components in tension and the verticals in compression. The hip verticals immediately adjacent to the inclined end posts of the bridge were generally not under a great deal of compression or tension. This design allowed longer bridges (up to 250 feet long) which could handle heavier loads. Later versions of the design added additional components to spread the forces. This design was very popular because it was easy to build and its cost was relatively low. The design wasn't replaced until stronger concrete deck designs were introduced that supplied more vertical clearance.

The trusses arrived at the bridge site during January 1891, and the bridge was erected in the spring of 1891. When finished, the seven-panel, pin-connected Pratt through truss bridge had a 126-foot span and was a total of 131 feet long. *The Morrilton Pilot* newspaper (April 3, 1891) reported that "the iron bridge at Friar's Ford is a beautiful structure." Note the spelling in the newspaper. At the time, the most recent census showed the family name spelling as including Fryer, Frier, Friar and Fryar.

Initially, the bridge made Fryer Bridge Road the main route between what became Arkansas Highways 95 (to the west) and Arkansas Highway 9 (to the east). Slowly, the road became less important and the bridge survived. Still, there was some activity in the area. A popular swimming hole was just downstream of the bridge, and the road developed the reputation of being a lovers' lane. There is also a legend that Fryer's Ford Bridge is haunted by the ghost of an outlaw's horse that was tethered there during the murders of the Richard Fryer family in April 1915.

The Solgohachia Murders

This photo is part of the Historic American Engineering Record (HAER) report about the Fryer's Ford Bridge, produced in 2005. The HAER is administered by the National Park Service and documents historically significant engineering sites and structures in the United States. *Fryer's Ford Bridge, Spanning East Fork of Point Remove Creek at Fryer Bridge Road CR 67, Solgohachia, Conway County, AR. 1968.* Historic American Engineering Record, Creator, Wrought Iron Bridge Company, David Hammond, Alfred Cook, W R Reeves, John Abbott, American Bridge Company, Thomas Pratt, and Caleb Pratt. Documentation compiled after. Photograph. https://www.loc.gov/item/ar0136/.

A series of small caves in Fryer Bluff (also known as Fryer's Bluff), located just west of the bridge, were also a local attraction. There is an old story told about these bluffs, which are on the south side of Pigeon Roost Mountain. The story states that during the late 1800s, a young Cherokee man came to Solgohachia. His handsome and exotic looks attracted a great deal of attention from area ladies, and his hard work made him a part of the community. One day, he got in a fight at Morrilton and killed a man. He claimed that it was self-defense, but had to flee to the caves in the area to hide. One of the young ladies of the community brought him food, and several people said that he worked in the area dressed like a woman. The young man eventually fled to Oklahoma, but was charged there with a crime against a woman, losing the last of his support in Solgohachia.

The caves were also a favorite location for the Fryer family. Gladys Fryer would speak about how she and her friends would play in those caves, especially during the summer when they were cool. During a visit towards the end of her life, she looked up at them and tried to see if she could still climb up to the caves.

This view of Fryer Bluff shows only a few of the caves that are found here. Photo by Barton Jennings.

By the 1970s, the Fryer family had mostly moved out of the area and the bridge was being called the Solgohachia Bridge by many. The Pratt through truss was becoming a rare structure in Arkansas, and around the country, and the Fryer Ford Bridge was placed on the National Register of Historic Places on May 26, 2004 (some sources state 1978). In 2005, the bridge was studied by the National Park Service (NPS) as part of the Historic American Engineering Record. The NPS report stated that at the time, Fryer's

Ford Bridge was "the oldest in-service bridge – and the second-oldest bridge of any type – in the State of Arkansas. It is an intact example of a pin-connected Pratt through truss, a type that is growing increasingly rare." The Arkansas State Highway and Transportation Department added that it was the oldest of twelve Pratt through truss bridges still standing in Arkansas.

Conway County still signs the road across East Fork Point Remove Creek as Fryer Bridge Road. Photo by Barton Jennings.

While a part of the history of Arkansas, the old Fryer's Ford Bridge is now gone, replaced by a more modern concrete and steel structure. The road is still known as Fryer Bridge Road, but also is designated as Conway County Road 67. Being a short route between Arkansas Highways

9 and 95, and with the boom in natural gas drilling in the area, it wasn't long before an over-weight truck tried to use the bridge. On April 11, 2011, a 9-ton truck tried to cross the bridge, which at the time had a 3-ton rating. Additionally, part of the load caught on a clearance bar, helping to tear down the Pratt through truss span. The west end of the bridge landed in the creek, in what was described as a mangled mess.

A large rain soon afterwards brought large amounts of debris against the bridge, and it formed a dam. The bridge was shoved further downstream and most of the components were twisted, bent, stretched or torn. While studies were conducted to repair the structure, it was too damaged and a new concrete bridge was built to keep the road open. Although the new bridge is much less scenic, the east end does feature a historic plaque that provides a brief history of the Fryer's Ford Bridge.

The new concrete Fryer Bridge certainly doesn't have the historic look of the earlier steel span, but it can now handle the heavier traffic that uses Fryer Bridge Road. Photo by Barton Jennings.

This small historical plaque about Fryer Bridge can be found on the east end of the new structure. Photo by Barton Jennings.

The Family Tragedy of April 26, 1915

Samuel Payton "Sam" Bell was a local cattle buyer who began dating Floy Maye Fryer, the second eldest of the Fryer daughters, about 1912. Bell's first love was apparently Maye's older sister Abbie, who he dated several times before she started dating Earl Bearden, a classmate of Bell's. There was some concern that Bell was simply going after another Fryer daughter as a way to stay close to Abbie, and Bell reportedly told a few people that he felt the Fryers were trying to run him off.

There were also some questions about Sam Bell's stability, as he had held a number of jobs since he had been orphaned at age 12 in 1899. Over the next decade, some relatives helped him while others married and handled their own families. He was raised by an older brother (Hugh – born in 1874) and sister (Salie – born in 1878). An older sister, Frances (born 1873), had married Dennis Q. Stell in 1890 and didn't take Sam Bell into her home. Sam was on his own by about 1910 as Hugh married in 1909 and Salie in 1911. Hugh married Birdie S. Stell, the daughter of the half-brother (Christopher Columbus Stell) of Dennis Stell. Salie became the second wife of Edward Lewis Tiner, who later testified against Sam Bell in his murder trials.

The general description of Sam Bell was that he was a cattle buyer, but he had also held several jobs in Morrilton, including as a salesman. He also took odd jobs on area farms. Despite not having the most stable upbringing, Sam Bell generally impressed people at a first meeting. Some of his family and friends seemed to be extremely loyal to him. However, over time many people, including some of his family, would start questioning some of his motives, and even his sanity. This seemed to apply to his courtship of Maye Fryer.

In July 1913, Sam and Maye applied for a marriage license. The paperwork included the strange statement "Do Not Publish." On July 31, 1913, the two were married and moved into a rented house on the farm of Moss Lafayette Miller, friends of the Fryer family. Even as they settled into the house, there were already concerns about the marriage. Sam Bell presented himself well in public, but he was known to have a temper, and he was soon taking it out on Maye. Members of the Fryer, Bearden and Bell families were upset about her treatment and tried to protect her. Despite the pleas, Sam's behavior only got worse and the Fryer and Bearden families – particularly Erdie and Abbie Bearden – moved Maye back to the Fryer farm by November. There, she reportedly required medical treatment for her injuries. A divorce followed in 1914, only seven months after the marriage.

Even before the divorce was final, the verbal attacks continued, if not increased, with threats of physical violence. Several times, Bell approached members of the Fryer and Bearden family at the store and post office in Solgohachia. In one noted case, Bell approached Abbie at the post office and made an explicit sexual proposition. Abbie responded angrily, and the incident was one of a number that were later brought up in Bell's trial. Dick Fryer, the father of Abbie and Maye, finally stepped in and warned Sam to stay away from Maye and the rest of the family. With this, Bell began to tell people that the Fryer family was the cause of the divorce, had threatened him, and had "dared him to come back to Solgohachia." Despite this, or maybe because of this, things got worse.

During February 1914, Bell marched back and forth through Solgohachia cursing Abbie for her support of Maye, for stealing his mail, and for all sorts of indecent activities. Erdie naturally defended his wife, and had a warrant issued for Bell's arrest. Even while being arrested, Bell shouted that he would "get Abbie and Dick Fryer if it took twenty years." He added that he would also kill the entire Bearden family and others who opposed him.

The arrest didn't stop Bell, who a few days later had a fight with Roy Fryer, Abbie's older brother. Later that day, Bell attacked Erdie when his back was turned, pulled a knife or razor (stories differ on the blade used) and tried to slice Bearden's throat, resulting in Erdie's neck and face being cut. The biggest gash ran from Erdie's mouth to his left ear. Again, Bell was arrested but soon released.

It wasn't just the Fryer family that Sam Bell was mad at. According to court records, Bell felt that some in his own family were supporting Maye and the Fryer family against him. He specifically mentioned a brother, sister, and uncle, whom he also threatened to kill. As stated in the case involving the Arkansas Supreme Court, Bell had "censured his own sister, who had raised him, accusing her of being a bitter enemy against him in his troubles...that before this time he had always spoken of her in terms of the tenderest affection; that he likewise censured his own brother, stating that his brother accused him of being crazy; also he had censured his uncle, and with both of these before that time he had been on affectionate terms; that he threatened to kill his own people and his wife's people, accusing them all of having turned against him and having ruined his life." As Bell made threats, even more members of his family spoke out against him, and he added a distant aunt, Ella Bell Brown, to his list of those who were against him. He also confronted Fred Brown, a cousin who operated a store in Plumerville. Fred had apparently told Sam that his actions could be part of the problem. Bell responded that Fred's statements had done him a grave injustice, with the message delivered in a threatening manner. Additionally, some witnesses reported that the Bearden family and neighbors were afraid for their lives. Basically, anyone who didn't fully support Bell's ideas was added to his enemies list.

Bell apparently had some political influence, and in spite of being arrested at least once for his assaults upon members of the Fryer and Bearden families, he was apparently never tried by a court and was free to roam the countryside. There were many reports of Sam Bell shadowing family members as they traveled about, and he seemed to always be at the stores in Solgohachia whenever a Fryer was there. Some of these meetings resulted in threats by Bell to kill the entire Fryer and Bearden families.

There were numerous cases of public conflict between Sam Bell and the Fryer family. In particular, much of the conflict was between Bell and Abbie Fryer, as well as her husband Erdie Bearden, and his brother Hugh Bearden. With Abbie working as the Solgohachia postmaster, and Hugh and Erdie running the J. W. Bearden and Sons' General Mercantile, the three were often together in town. Abbie had been very supportive of her younger sister Maye, and Bell stated publicly several times that Abbie and Erdie were the cause of the conflict with his wife. Several Solgohachia residents later testified that Bell had publicly insulted various women of the Fryer family, especially Abbie. For example, just a few months before the divorce, Bell had approached Abbie at the post office and made a strong sexual suggestion, which she loudly rejected. Hugh, who was in the post office, later stated that Abbie "upbraided him bitterly."

However, through late 1914, Bell started spending less time at Solgohachia, generally living in the Plumerville area. Records show that he was living with the William Lacefield family near Plumerville by December 1914. There, he helped around the Lacefield farm and apparently held a few odd jobs. Nevertheless, the list of his enemies grew as various members of his own family began to question his actions, with some even saying that it was his temper that had run off Maye. Several later described him as being unbalanced. By early 1915, almost anyone who ran into Sam Bell would hear from him his latest threats and promises of murder. A network to warn family members seemed to have been organized, and few people went to town when Bell was around.

The Murders of April 26th

In mid-April of 1915, Bell seemed to have made a decision about something, and was described as calm and relaxed by the Lacefields. He had earlier written a long love letter to Maye, which she ignored. The letter described dreams that he had about reuniting with Maye, and asked her to meet with him in private as he was afraid of the Fryer family. Maye's failure to respond had caused a few fits of anger and crying, but Bell seemed to be taking it well. Nevertheless, on April 24th, it was noted that Bell left the Lacefield house with his shotgun, apparently returning later without it.

The conflict came to a peak on Monday, April 26, 1915. The event was described as follows in several newspapers. "In a wholesale murder at Solgohachia, 10 miles north of Morrilton, about 8 o'clock tonight, Sam Bell, a young cattle buyer, killed his father-in-law, Dick Fryer; his brother-in-law, Amos Fryer; his sister-in-law, Mrs. Earl Bearden; and her husband." The cause was reportedly the recent divorce between Bell and his wife, Floy Maye Fryer. Bell felt that the Fryer family had encouraged his wife to leave him and obtain the divorce. It was clear that Sam Bell had been abusive to his wife, and several Fryer and Bearden family members had threatened Bell if he kept beating Maye, and then encouraged her to leave when he didn't stop.

Details about that night can be found in numerous newspapers, court records, and from the stories of Fryer and Bearden family members, as well as neighbors. The day was a typical warm spring day, and farmers and ranchers in the Arkansas River Valley were dealing with the typical round of spring flooding, which provided many of the newspaper headlines that month. The evening was pleasant and a full moon would be in the sky.

Bell had gone to Plumerville that morning, returning to the Lacefield house early in the afternoon. He ate and then worked with William Lacefield in planting crops on his farm. He never returned to the Lacefield home, instead taking his horse to look at some cattle that were on the market. Along the way, he stopped at the Raymer farm to discuss some of their cattle that were for sale. The discussion didn't seem to be unusual, and Mary Raymer described him as being "in a perfectly even frame of mind." He then approached the Erdie Bearden house and tied the horse up. Some sources state that he tied his horse up near the Fryer Ford Bridge. However, this was several miles from the home of Erdie and Abbie. Several small streams did flow under the road near their home, and he could have tied his horse to one of these bridges. Court records simply stated that he tied the horse up near the Bearden house, with some newspapers stating that the "animal was tied about two hundred yards from the house."

It was growing dark at Solgohachia. Sunset had been a little before 7pm, but a full moon was coming up, providing enough light to see. This was before the era of streetlights, but most area homes had indoor lighting using lamps. Since Bell knew the area, it wasn't hard for him to navigate through the community.

The Family Tragedy of April 26, 1915

The home of Erdie and Abbie was on the main road west from Solgohachia to Fryer's Ford Bridge, almost across the street from the home of Paul Gordon. For years, this was the main road west, but much of it has been realigned since the early 1900s. The house was on the south side of what is currently known as Doe Road, located a short distance to the northeast from the current intersection with Solgohachia Road (County Road 67). Nothing remains of the house except for a small level spot in the brush.

Solgohachia Road is currently the main Conway County road that heads west from Solgohachia, Arkansas. Photo by Barton Jennings.

Doe Drive is part of what was once the main road west from Solgohachia. It was along Doe Drive that the murders of four innocent members of the Fryer and Bearden family took place. Photo by Barton Jennings.

The home of Richard T. Fryer was several hundred yards to the west, located on what had once been Road District No. 1 of Washington Township, now known as Solgohachia Road. The 1910 census report stated that the home of Richard T. Fryer was at "Salgachi and Hotwells Road." The house was on the north side of the road, just west of the intersection of today's Solgohachia and Doe roads. The remains of a stone wall, some huge trees, and an old house mark the location. This placed both houses less than a half-mile from Solgohachia. The properties of various Fryer family members were scattered along the old highway to the west side of the East Fork of Point Remove Creek. Several other families, such as the Gordons and the Atkinsons, also had homes and farms throughout this area.

The Family Tragedy of April 26, 1915

After he left his horse behind, Bell quietly walked up to the home of Erdie and Abbie Bearden, who were sitting down for dinner. Newspaper reports indicate that Bell planned his arrival carefully, even bringing a pair of "carpet slippers" to allow a quiet approach. Apparently, Bell felt that the slippers were too noisy and he actually threw them away and walked barefoot to the Bearden home. He had publicly stated that he would shoot the Beardens through a window while they were having dinner, so his actions appeared to be well thought out.

Arriving at the house, Bell found Erdie and Abbie sitting down for dinner after a day working at the store and post office, and some on the farm. Erdie sat with his left side toward the window, with Abbie sitting across the table. Seeing this, Bell shot Erdie Bearden through the dining room window using a repeating shotgun. The left shoulder of Erdie was torn off, and he turned towards the window after being shot. A second shot from Bell then entered Erdie's heart, and death was apparently immediate. Erdie fell into the arms of his wife, Abbie, who had also received some of the shot in her abdomen. Her screams of pain and sorrow attracted the attention of much of the Fryer family, who were in the main house about 150 yards away. She was then shot twice, and screamed and staggered from the room. Newspapers reported initially that "the shot was not instantly fatal." However, Abbie apparently got no further than the doorway out of the dining room before falling to the ground.

There may have been a reason that Abbie was shot by Bell in her abdomen. At the time, Erdie and Abbie were trying to have a child and some rumors stated that she was possibly pregnant, carrying the child of her husband Erdie. Bell had publicly promised to exterminate the Fryer and Bearden families, and he was reportedly furious that Abbie and Erdie were happily married while his own wife had fled his home.

After murdering the two, Bell apparently ripped the latched screen door down, entered their house and looked around for others to shoot. No one was there, so he then destroyed some of the family's possessions before focusing on the main house. Abbie was still alive, and evidence taken at the scene showed that Bell had stomped on her face. Later, Bell claimed that he just covered her mouth to silence her screams so he could hear if anyone was approaching the house. There must have been some sort of understanding about the situation as Richard T. "Dick" Fryer grabbed a gun and headed toward his daughter's house, warning the rest of the family to flee. Meanwhile, Theresa Reiter Fryer started rounding up the family and getting them out of the back of the house. Family legend states that William Franklin "Jerry" Fryer was told that he was in charge as his older brother John Amos Fryer went upstairs to get his gun, and then followed his father out of the house.

Sam Bell had said for more than a year that he would kill all of the Fryer and Bearden family members, and he next took aim at Dick Fryer. At first, Bell hid in the darkened house of Erdie and Abbie, waiting for others to approach. He wedged a window open using its curtains so he would have a clear shot at anyone coming from the front of the house. As Dick Fryer was calling for Erdie and Abbie, Bell exited the Bearden house and stood on the dark porch. The two exchanged shots, with Fryer's rifle shot passing through a sleeve of Bell's coat, while Bell's shot hit Dick in the right arm. Dick Fryer was forced to reload his rifle, but Bell was able to shoot him through his side with his repeating shotgun. Despite the shot damaging his heart, Dick Fryer turned towards his house and walked about thirty yards before falling to the ground, dead.

The Family Tragedy of April 26, 1915

As Dick Fryer was staggering towards his home, Sam Bell was also heading that way. Before reaching the main house, he met Paul Gordon, a neighbor from across the road who had heard the shootings. Paul Gordon, the brother of one-time Solgohachia postmaster Arkansas "Arka" Gordon, had known Sam Bell for years. Gordon and Bell briefly talked, and while pointing his shotgun at Gordon, Bell told Paul that he "wouldn't harm a hair of your head." However, when Bell discovered that Paul Gordon was carrying a pistol, he ordered him to drop the pistol or have the top of his head shot off. Gordon dropped his pistol and fled to some nearby bushes, becoming a witness to some of Bell's actions and the final killing.

Paul Gordon stated that Bell then went to the body of Dick Fryer, grabbed his hair and raised his head, and then laughed while yelling "The old man's dead." Bell kept laughing until he saw John Amos Fryer approach. Bell then "started toward him gritting his teeth so that it could be heard a distance of thirty feet." Paul Gordon stated that he yelled at Amos to warn him of the danger. However, within moments, both Amos and Bell fired at about the same time, and Amos dropped dead from only one shot.

As the shooting was underway, most of the Fryer family, including Maye, fled the main house and hid in the nearby fields, probably saving their lives. About the same time, Theresa Reiter Fryer headed out of the house to determine what had happened to her husband, daughter and son. Several family members – principally Roy and Jerry – grabbed her and tried to take her away. Bell saw them and started their way. He fired another shot at them, slightly wounding another one of the Fryer sons, and possibly Theresa. Mrs. Fryer was taken to the home of J. M. Atkinson, where she and some of the family were hidden on the second floor.

After the Shootings

Bell continued looking for members of the Fryer family, but with other neighbors arriving on the scene, he apparently left the Fryer farm. Some newspaper reports stated that Bell was initially unfrightened by the appearance of neighbors and continued to search for Mrs. Fryer and her other children. After several minutes of searching for members of the Fryer family, and more neighbors arriving at the farm, Bell headed to his horse, where he encountered more neighbors who were guarding it.

He then headed to Morrilton on foot, located about ten miles away. Several newspapers reported that before Bell had gone 100 yards he met a neighbor carrying a shotgun. Bell forced this neighbor to drop the gun and then continued. Reports from those who saw him after the shooting stated that he seemed to be crazy, laughing a great deal and doing strange things. He never retrieved his horse or shoes, instead heading towards town barefoot, following what is today Arkansas Highway 9.

Some reports stated that Bell walked by the home of John and Margaret Bearden, the parents of Erdie. Their house was on the main highway to Morrilton, across from the Solgohachia cemetery. They also owned farmland that was adjacent to the Fryer's farm. Bell certainly walked by the homes of a number of neighbors, and in the still and quiet night, many had heard the shots and were out looking for the shooter. A number later stated that they knew the noise was Bell shooting Erdie and Abbie.

One of those who heard the shooting and knew what it meant was John Will Bearden, the father of Erdie. Before he could leave the house, the family's phone rang. Neighbors were already sharing the news about the shooting, and the Bearden's were quickly informed that Erdie had been shot. Another Bearden who was called was Fred Bearden,

The Family Tragedy of April 26, 1915

who worked as a doctor at Morrilton. Fred loaded up his family in his car and rushed to Solgohachia.

Somewhere on his walk Bell passed the car of Fred Bearden, the brother of Erdie. Along with Deputy Sheriff Hall Morrell, Fred was heading to the shooting as he was a physician and county coroner. Bearden family stories state that Fred Bearden actually had his wife and family with him as he rushed to Solgohachia. When he arrived at the Fryer farm, Fred Bearden had his wife Glenna lie down on the front seat and his children to lie on the floorboards. It was obvious that he was worried about Bell's threats to also exterminate the Bearden family and he wanted to protect his wife and children.

When Fred Bearden arrived at the scene, he found that Abbie had been moved to a bed to comfort her. Some who were there reported that Abbie had remained conscious for a few minutes, asking people to loosen her corset, part of which had been blown into her side. She died within 30 minutes of being shot. Fred also found that Erdie, Dick and Amos had been shot and killed. After a full inspection, Fred took his family back to Morrilton, again passing Sam Bell, who stated that he would hide in the woods whenever a car went by.

While Bell walked towards Morrilton, law enforcement and neighbors were on the hunt for him. The *Arkansas Gazette* (April 27, 1915) reported that "Bell escaped and though officers and posses are searching the woods, no trace of the murderer had been found at a late hour…It is expected that if they locate the fugitive the officers will have a desperate encounter in capturing Bell. He is considered a very dangerous character."

Bell had lived and worked in Morrilton and was known by a number of people. When he arrived in town, Bell met several residents who later stated that he was looking for Sheriff Gordon. He actually woke the owner of a wagon

The Solgohachia Murders

yard and had him provide a ride, but ordered the driver to stop two blocks short of the sheriff's house. Bell then walked past the residence of the sheriff and woke up others asking for directions. One of these was R. L "Bob" Greer, who previously had employed Bell at his clothing and shoe store in Morrilton. At first, Greer didn't know why Bell had awakened him. However, as they chatted in Greer's living room, Bell began to tell the story of how he had killed Erdie, Abbie, Dick and Amos. Greer later stated that when Bell would speak of the most gruesome parts of the murders, he would start laughing, described as a short but harsh laugh. Bell also told Greer that he had been thinking of suicide, but that "I can't afford to die and leave them living." Bob Greer helped to convince Bell to surrender, and stated that Bell kept talking about suicide. He also asked several times if electrocution was painful. One of Greer's biggest challenges was getting Bell to leave his shotgun behind. From the description, he seemed to hang on to it like a crutch or life preserver.

Bell found out that his friend Sheriff James Monroe Gordon (brother of Paul Gordon) was out of town. In reality, Sheriff James Gordon and all of his deputies, except for James Earl, had already gone to the scene of the shooting and were looking for Bell. Bob Greer walked with Bell as he headed through Morrilton, and he eventually surrendered to Deputy Sheriff James G. Earl at 1:30am. Bell spoke to the deputy sheriff and told him of the killings, but showed no concern or remorse. The deputy sheriff, who had known Sam Bell "intimately" for many years, later said that his clothes were soiled but that Bell seemed to be at peace with his actions. In fact, the sheriff reported that he could not tell that Bell was acting any differently than when he "was at peace with everybody." Bell did continue to laugh "a hacking laugh" as he described the shooting, and even asked the sheriff if he thought that he would be electrocuted. Bell, Greer and Earl then went to the jail in the county courthouse.

After his arrest, Bell reportedly refused to talk to his attorney who had represented him before on at least one other case. To protect Bell from a potential lynch mob, Deputy Earl moved him on the 5am train to the Pulaski County jail in Little Rock. Apparently, Bell did talk to a few people on the train as *The Log Cabin Democrat* (Tuesday, April 27, 1915) reported that "Parties who saw him pass through Conway this morning say he declared he was ready to go to the electric chair, but regretted that he did not get to kill a certain Plumerville man." The Plumerville man was likely his uncle, one of several family members that Bell claimed had turned on him for no reason.

Despite the end of the shootings, most of the story had just begun. Late on Tuesday, April 27th, a funeral was held at the Solgohachia Friendship Cemetery for the four victims of Sam Bell's actions. The Solgohachia Friendship Cemetery had a direct connection to the Bearden family. Most of the first people buried there were members of the Bearden family, placed here 1886-1894. Later, John Will Bearden, Erdie's father, donated the land for the community cemetery.

Reverend R. E. L. Bearden, Sr., presiding elder of the Conway district, officiated at the funerals, and more than 1000 "farmers and their families from all sections of the county" attended the burial. The bodies of Erdie and Abbie (Barbra Abagail) Bearden were buried together in one grave while the bodies of Dick and Amos Fryer were buried in another. The two graves were located near each other, and are today near the center of the cemetery. The cemetery was directly across the road from the John Bearden house and next to his orchard, and family members had to look at the grave markers for as long as they lived in the house.

This sign along Arkansas Highway 9 marks the Solgohachia Friendship Community Cemetery, the final resting place of Erdie, Abbie, Dick and Amos. Photo by Barton Jennings.

The graves of Margaret and John Will Bearden are in the family section of the Solgohachia Friendship Community Cemetery, near those of the Fryer family. Photo by Barton Jennings.

Even before the funerals, members of the Fryer family received the support of neighbors. Besides the Atkinson family, the Dillon family harbored some of the Fryer family at their home in Morrilton. Soon after the funerals, a series of legal cases began that would determine the future of the shooter, and the safety of the Fryer and Bearden families, and even some members of the Bell family. These would last for years and would often be the first of their kind, with some including the Arkansas Supreme Court.

On April 28th, the coroner's inquest was held at Solgohachia, with Fred Bearden reportedly stepping aside and letting others handle the inquest for his brother Erdie and Erdie's wife Abbie. The findings quickly were sent to the Fifth Judicial Circuit and the proper prosecuting attorneys. Within several weeks, legal action would begin.

The Victims

The shootings of April 26, 1915, caused the death of three members of the Fryer family and one member of the Bearden family. Three of the four were young, in their teens and twenties. These deaths create an unusual cluster of graves in the Solgohachia Friendship Community Cemetery, all with the same date of death. Over the years, these dates have provided a hint to visitors that something horrible happened at Solgohachia.

The four victims of the shooting were buried late the next day (April 27, 1915) at the Solgohachia Friendship Cemetery, located south of downtown Solgohachia. The funeral demonstrated some of the importance of the Fryer and Bearden families. Fred Bearden, Erdie's older brother, was a physician and the Conway County coroner who released the bodies to the families for burial. Presiding was a very distant relative, Reverend Robert Edward Lee Bearden, Sr., a noted Arkansas Methodist minister. (Years later, Tomme, my mother and a daughter of Gladys, attended Central Methodist Church in Fayetteville, Arkansas, where Reverend Robert Edward Lee Bearden, Jr., preached.) More than 1000 "farmers and their families from all sections of the county" attended the burial. The bodies of Erdie and Abbie, husband and wife, were buried together in one grave while the bodies of Dick and his son Amos were buried in another. The two graves were located near each other at the center of the cemetery.

The following is a bit of the history of those buried that day in the cemetery.

Erdie Bearden (1886-1915)

The first person shot that terrible evening was Erdie Bearden. Erdie was named Earl at birth, but known as Erdie by many. In more formal transactions, he was Eard, sometimes spelled simply Erd. The marriage license was signed Eard while the cemetery marker uses Erdie.

Erdie married Barbara Abagail "Abbie" Fryer on Christmas Day in 1910, and became a loved member of the Fryer family. He helped on the Fryer farm and worked at the Bearden store in Solgohachia. Erdie was born on September 24, 1886, to John Will Bearden (1858-1943) and Margaret E. Haynes Bearden (1863-1949). Like many area residents, the Bearden family moved to Arkansas during the early 1800s from eastern states. In this case, the Beardens arrived from Spartanburg County, South Carolina, between 1853 and 1859. Reverend Berryman Hicks Bearden (1825-1894) and his wife Harriet N. Smith Bearden (1823-1897) moved to Arkansas, and the reverend helped to organize the Missionary Baptist Church of Lewisburg in 1860. One of their children was John Will Bearden, the father of Erdie Bearden. As described in a history of Conway County, John Will Bearden was born in Arkansas and at an early age began farming in Conway County. He married Margaret E. Haynes and became "one of the prominent agriculturists of the county and in addition to general farming raises a fine grade of live stock." The family also operated a store at Solgohachia – the J. W. Bearden and Sons' General Mercantile.

The Family Tragedy of April 26, 1915

Erdie was close to the Fryer family and was often photographed with them. This photo is of Amos Fryer and Erdie Bearden, apparently just a short time before the shootings. Photo from the collection of Tomme Jennings.

Erdie was the second son and he was engaged in the mercantile business in Solgohachia. The store that he worked at was managed (some sources say owned) by his younger brother Homer. Homer, born in 1888, opened the store by 1913 and was also admitted to the bar in 1915, although he seldom practiced that profession. He also taught in the schools of Solgohachia. Homer Bearden was later an important witness on behalf of the State in the murder trials against Sam Bell as a number of threats had been made by Bell against the Fryer and Bearden families at his store.

Erdie was described as handsome, standing six feet tall. His younger brother Roby later described him as "quick, strong, and resourceful, with a sly sense of humor." Like Abbie, Erdie had fair hair, but he was also known for his blue eyes. While named Earl, he used the name Eard on the marriage license. Why Erdie, Eard and even Erd? The Bearden family claims that Fred Bearden, a brother less than two years older, couldn't say Earl and would instead say Eard or Erdie.

Homer Bearden was an important witness on behalf of the State in the murder trials. When he passed away, he was buried near his family and the grave site of Erdie and Abbie. Photo by Barton Jennings.

The Family Tragedy of April 26, 1915

Barbara Abagail Fryer (1892-1915)

During the 1910s, changes were also taking place within the Fryer family. Barbara Abagail Fryer (Barbra in many family records and known as Sister Abby or Abbie) was the oldest daughter (born on March 23, 1892) and was helping to run the household. By 1909, she was also the Solgohachia postmaster. Abbie was described as being one of the most beautiful girls in the region. Stories stated that her light brown hair graced her softly rounded face. She had fair skin and brown eyes, but was also described as being skilled at cooking, running a household, and having plenty of business sense.

She was reportedly popular in school, and a number of young men seemed interested in courting her. However, on Christmas Day in 1910, Erdie Bearden and Barbara Fryer were married in the home of Richard T. Fryer, her father. They moved into a home on part of the Fryer farm, located about 150 yards away from that of her parents and less than a mile from the home of Erdie's parents. Abbie, then officially known as Mrs. Barbara A. Bearden by the postal service, was still shown as postmaster in 1911 with a $130 compensation. She also apparently helped out at the adjacent Bearden store in Solgohachia, where a number of confrontations with Sam Bell took place.

Abbie was the one who helped to organize the Fryer and Bearden families in an attempt to save Maye from Sam Bell. While noted by some as being small compared to her husband, she was also described as being determined in her defense of Maye and the rest of her family. While she was the second one shot, Abbie was the last to die. She spoke to several people, providing a few details about the shooting. A local neighbor, H. M. Williams, was the first to enter the Bearden house after the shooting, and he found the mortally wounded Abbie. He stated that she asked him to remove her corset because the stays had been blown into her side by the shotgun blast. Others quickly arrived and she received some comfort and was moved to a bed, where Dr. Fred Bearden found her. She held on for about thirty minutes before dying from her wounds.

This marker in the Solgohachia Friendship Community Cemetery marks the graves of Erdie and Abbie Bearden. Note the spelling of the names, Erdie instead of Eard, and Barbra Abagail instead of Abbie. Photo by Sarah Jennings.

Richard Thomas "Dick" Fryer (1860-1915)

My great-grandfather, Richard Thomas "Dick" Fryer, was born on September 17, 1860, in Conway County, Arkansas. When his father Jeremiah Fryer died in 1872, Richard Fryer became the head of the household at age 11. This leadership soon extended beyond his family and he took on several community roles throughout his life.

The Family Tragedy of April 26, 1915

One major sign of his independence was his October 14, 1888, marriage to Theresa Reiter. This was a marriage that violated the demands of both his family and the family of Theresa. Theresa Reiter was born in Grossarl, Austria, on October 12, 1868, and her first decade was spent in the "old world." Immigration reports showed that she and all of the other children in her family had blue eyes and blond hair, very different from the local population made up of decedents of English, Scottish, Irish, French, and other non-Nordic countries. Additionally, the arrival of many Roman Catholics from Germany and Austria created some conflicts in the area, as most of the earlier settlers followed various Protestant faiths, especially Methodism. This hard feeling was apparently especially true between the Methodist Fryer and Catholic Reiter families.

Family legend has Theresa, generally known as Thresa, and Richard falling in love despite the religious and cultural problems between the two families. To end the relationship, the Reiter family sent Thresa to Fort Smith, Arkansas, to be a housekeeper. Somehow, the relationship continued, and Richard traveled to Fort Smith and married Thresa on October 14, 1888.

The marriage was apparently between two strong-willed individuals, and the battle between the two families reportedly ended due to their insistence. Ten children came out of the marriage, including the author's grandmother. These children were Roy Thomas (1890-1962), Barbara Abagail (1892-1915), Porter Henry (1894-1973), Floy Maye (1896-1964), John Amos (1898-1915), William Franklin (1900-1987), Thresa Gladys (1903-1999), Willie Bernice (1905-2001), James Dwight (1908-1974), and Richard Elmo (1911-1946). In addition, there was an infant who was born and died on July 9, 1889.

This photo shows Dick and Theresa with their five oldest children, Roy and Abbie on the back row, with Maye, Amos and Porter on the front row. Photo from the collection of Tomme Jennings.

After a few years, members of the Reiter family began to move further west, generally to Oklahoma. Those that stayed generally lived in area Catholic communities like St. Vincent, but maintained ties with the Fryer family. However, one challenge reported by a family member is that they generally spoke only German, so communications were difficult. On February 2, 1908, Barbara Weber Reiter died at Saint Vincent, Arkansas, a few miles northwest of the Fryer farm on today's Arkansas Highway 95. She was buried in the Saint Mary's Cemetery at Saint Vincent, where a number of members of the Reiter family were also buried. Her husband, John Reiter, moved to Oklahoma to join much of the family and passed away at Wanette, in Pottawatomie County, Oklahoma, on April 11, 1923.

The Family Tragedy of April 26, 1915

Barbara Weber Reiter, the mother of Theresa Reiter Fryer, was buried in the Saint Vincent Cemetery, located near the St. Mary Catholic Church. Photo by Barton Jennings.

Meanwhile, Dick, often documented as Richard T., or more simply R. T., had grown the farm and was often cited as being one of the "most respected citizens of Conway County." In a 1909 listing of post office officials, R. T. Fryer was listed as the clerk of the Solgohachia post office.

In the same government report, Barbara A. Fryer was shown as the postmaster. On the Fryer family farm along Point Remove Creek, several homes had been built for the families of some of the children. Changes were taking place in the community, county and state as industry and manufacturing increased, farming was under pressure, and better transportation reached the Solgohachia community. It seems that the Fryer and Bearden families were positioning themselves to succeed in the changing environment. However, some of the plans were changed due to efforts to first save Maye from Sam Bell, and then to avoid his presence and threats. Dick began to keep his rifle close by, and was killed within a few minutes of the first shots as he headed to the home of his daughter in an attempt to protect her and the rest of his family.

Few photos of Dick Fryer without the rest of his family are known to exist. This one is reportedly of Dick standing in his crop of corn, near his home. This is probably the corn field where several members of the Fryer family hid in the stubble the horrible night of April 26, 1915. Photo from the collection of Tomme Jennings.

The Family Tragedy of April 26, 1915

This traditional Woodmen of the World tree trunk monument marks the final resting place of Richard Thomas "Dick" Fryer. Heavily weathered, a light cleaning has allowed the name and wording to be read by those who pass by. Photo by Barton Jennings.

John Amos Fryer (1898-1915)

The fourth person shot and killed the evening of April 26th was John Amos Fryer. Known simply as Amos by the family, John was born on March 27, 1898, and had turned 17 the month before he was shot and killed. At the time, Amos was the oldest son regularly living in the main house, so it was his job to support his dad, which is what got him killed. Amos reportedly spent most of his time working on the farm, especially since his father had some work at the post office in town.

Amos was known for his pranks and sense of humor. The few photos of him show him smiling and often playing games with other family members. The Moss Miller family's history states that Amos was the sweetheart of Lois Lucille Miller, who lived on a nearby farm at Solgohachia.

This photo of Amos Fryer was apparently taken shortly before his death. He was a known prankster, and appears to be hiding a young lady from the camera. Could this possibly be Lois Miller? Photo from the collection of Tomme Jennings.

The Family Tragedy of April 26, 1915

This small marker for Amos Fryer stands next to the large Richard T. Fryer marker in Solgohachia Friendship Community Cemetery. Photo by Barton Jennings.

The Solgohachia Murders

The Trials and Years of Frustration

As stated in William Shakespeare's *Julius Caesar*: "The evil that men do lives after them." Seldom has this been more true than the impact of the many trials, escapes and furloughs of Sam Bell, and the repercussions upon the surviving Fryer and Bearden family members. Even today, long after the deaths of everyone involved, the murders of April 26, 1915, still haunt members of the families. In some ways, it has also haunted the legal system of the State of Arkansas.

The several trials and court rulings that followed the murders deserve a book in themselves, and have been used as teaching tools by the Harvard Law School and others. The killings involved some of the most important families in Conway County – the Fryer, Bearden, and Gordon families had all intermarried and members held various positions within the communities. In addition, there were the Bells, also once a well-known family.

The Bell, Bearden and Fryer families were also actually related through marriage. On January 3, 1908, William Merle Bearden, a younger brother of Erdie and Homer, had married Myrtle Elinor Stell. Myrtle was the daughter of Frances Bell, the oldest sister of Sam Bell, and Dennis Q. Stell. This created a number of potential conflicts of loyalty within the various families, plus ways to pass messages among the family members. Some of these connections are probably what led Sam Bell to declare that some members of his own family had turned against him.

This book is designed to be about the Fryer family, not Sam Bell. Unfortunately, he has impacted the family for more than 100 years. Yes, there is hatred inside and outside the family for Sam Bell, and his name really shouldn't be repeated as often as is necessary to describe the criminal cases. Because of this, a simple "SB" will be used throughout this chapter.

The initial news reports, made by phone from Solgohachia and Morrilton, included statements about officers searching for "SB" near the scene of the crime, but he did eventually surrender to Deputy Sheriff J. G. Earl the early morning after the murders. After "SB" finally found the deputy sheriff at Morrilton, he was arrested and held in the local jail. "SB" seemed to have received some favoritism as he was never handcuffed, but instead moved to the Pulaski County jail in Little Rock for his protection, with law officers worried about a public lynching. He was placed on St. Louis, Iron Mountain & Southern train No. 105, the *Texas & Louisiana Express*, an overnight express and sleeper train which was scheduled to depart Morrilton at 4:53am and arrive at Little Rock at 7:00am.

While being processed at Little Rock, it was discovered that "SB" had never been searched and that he was still carrying a .38 caliber revolver that he apparently planned to use on himself as part of a planned murder-suicide. This happened despite warnings to the public that he was armed and considered to be a very dangerous character, and had previously attempted to kill Erdie Bearden with a knife.

"SB" was allowed to sleep at the Pulaski County jail, but eventually was interviewed by both law officers and the press. His initial comments were "I have nothing to say at all," then "I am ready to die," and finally "I wish I was dead." He then refused to talk to anyone. Over the next few days, a number of news articles were published across the country, many that included interviews with "SB". However, none included interviews with the Fryer family. Because of this, many of the articles focused on the suffering of "SB" as he awaited his fate. Always described as a successful Conway

County cattle buyer, much was made of his good looks and good manners. Several examples follow from the *Arkansas Gazette* (April 28, 1915).

> *Bell is not of the common criminal type. He is intelligent, speaks correct English and although he refused talk of his crime to a Gazette reporter at the jail yesterday afternoon, he spoke very courteously and made it plain that he did not wish to give offense.*
>
> *He would afford an interesting subject for a student of psychology – this big, boyish-looking son of the soil that admittedly is guilty of one of the most bloody crimes in the annals of Arkansas, who killed four persons and shot at a fifth.*
>
> *His countenance is intelligence, his conversation shows that he possesses more intellect than the average man of his type, his politeness and courtesy contradict the brutality that one must associate with his fearful crime, and there is no hint of sullenness in his manner – only an yielding reserve and determination to keep his counsel.*

Later, reporters began to question the actions of "SB" and whether some of it was just a show. The *Arkansas Gazette* reported on June 12th that: "Either Sam Bell is possessed of a mentality that sets him apart from the rest of the human race, or he is one of the greatest actors the world has ever seen." The paper also stated that he was "one of the strangest of his race who has ever figured in the criminal annals of Arkansas."

The Solgohachia Murders

Meanwhile, in a discussion with another inmate, "SB" admitted his guilt and stated that he didn't want to beat the charges. He spoke little, and reportedly refused to talk to his attorney, who had represented him before on at least one other case. "SB" did once request that some of his family visit him, but he still refused to discuss the shootings. Despite his claims that he should be punished for the crimes, "SB" and his family already seemed to be planning a way out of the troubles.

One person that "SB" did seem to enjoy meeting was Reverend Lee Tomme, the chaplain of the Arkansas penitentiary. Reverend Tomme met with "SB" multiple times, and was sometimes described as being "Bell's spiritual advisor." It was reported that after a visit by Tomme that "SB" would become more calm. During several of these talks, it was clear that "SB" was fearful of his fate after death. He expressed the opinion "that his doom, from a spiritual standpoint, was sealed" because there was no hope for a murderer after death. Eventually "SB" asked to be baptized, apparently to save his soul after his execution. Even with this, "SB" refused to tell Reverend Tomme many of the details of the shootings, and didn't seem to feel remorse for his actions. However, one newspaper reported that "SB" did express some regret to Reverend Tomme that some of his victims might not have been prepared to die.

It should be noted that the series of murder trials involving "SB", and the rulings involved, established a number of legal definitions and precedents that impacted legal cases across the country. Some of these are still applied today. The Harvard Law School's Caselaw Access Project includes the *Bell v. State* case, handled by the Arkansas Supreme Court in November 1915. For those who want to understand the many legal issues with the case, a reading of the 33-page report is recommended. Details about the case are also found in *The Southwestern Reporter Volume*

180, which reported on supreme and appellate courts in Arkansas and other surrounding states.

Another review of the trials can be found from a report written by Joan Bearden Broening, available from the Morrilton Depot Museum and Genealogy Library. This 20-page report, simply entitled *April 26, 1915*, looks at the murder and legal case from the point of view of the Bearden Family. While several errors have been found, there is a great deal of accurate detail that makes interesting reading.

The Murder Trial for the Death of Eard Bearden

An investigation of the murders took place almost immediately, and on May 5, 1915, the Honorable M. L. Davis, judge of the Fifth Judicial Circuit, called a special term of the Conway Circuit Court to a Tuesday, May 18th session. As part of the hearing, Sheriff James Gordon brought "SB" back to Morrilton on Iron Mountain local train No. 104, which was scheduled to arrive at 10:08am. A huge crowd had gathered at the Morrilton train station, and for Bell's safety, he was unloaded from the rear of the train. From there, it was a fast walk for a single block to the courthouse, which avoided most of the crowd. The circuit court call recited that "SB" was accused of murder and was confined in jail, and that the call was made for the purpose of investigating and disposing of the charge. The charges were reported on and a grand jury was empaneled. Within 45 minutes of hearing the evidence, the grand jury returned four separate indictments against 'SB', all for first degree murder by shooting different persons.

The plan was to hold a separate trial for each of the four victims, but only if necessary. The general consensus was that "SB" would receive the death penalty at the first trial and further trials would not be necessary. Since the first person shot was Erdie, the first trial involved the murder of Eard Bearden.

"SB" didn't have an official attorney, so several were appointed to defend him. J. A. Eades of Morrilton was his primary attorney, with J. M. Henson of Leslie assisting. These attorneys were possibly chosen with the help of Hugh Bell, who was often the most vocal advocate for the defense. Hugh McElhannon "Mack" Bell (1874-1952) was more than a dozen years older than his younger brother "SB". After their parents died in 1899, Mack Bell took charge of the family and raised Sam, and seemed to be about his only vocal defender, although several of his three sisters reportedly wept throughout his trials. Hugh Bell worked with the attorneys throughout the trial, but as a number of newspapers reported, "at no time during the trial did Bell consent to talk to his lawyers." In fact, "SB" spoke to no one in the courtroom and his attorneys said that "he preserves complete and absolute silence concerning the tragedy."

The prosecution used a team of local and state prosecutors (Prosecuting Attorney A. S. Hayes, and Deputy Prosecutors J. B. Ward and V. G. Jordan), plus "specially employed counsel" Edward Gordon of Solgohachia, who knew most everyone involved with the case. In fact, he was the younger brother of Paul Gordon, who had met "SB" on the Fryer farm the night of the shooting. He was also the brother of Deputy Sheriff James Monroe Gordon, who "SB" attempted to surrender to the night of the shootings. In many reports from the time, Ed Gordon was described as being a well-known attorney at Morrilton.

On Thursday, May 20th, Judge Davis met with the prosecution and defense attorneys in preparation for the trial. At the time, the law required at least 48 hours between an indictment and a trial, so Friday, May 21st was chosen as the start of the trial for the murder of Eard Bearden. The trial began about 10am with the selection of a jury, and the courtroom was packed with more than 600 people, plus more in the surrounding hallways and outside lawns, listening through open doors and windows.

The trial quickly became complicated as the defense challenged any testimony and description of the murder scene that included the other victims. There were also challenges to the many witnesses that described the conflicts that happened before the murders, but who had no information about the shootings themselves. Eventually, a dozen witnesses for the prosecution told what they knew, including information about threats made by "SB" to kill the entire Fryer family. Among these witnesses were Homer Bearden, who described many of the threats against Eard; and Paul Gordon, who witnessed at least one shooting and "SB" celebrating the others; and M. W. Williams, who spoke about his conversation with the dying Abbie Bearden. The attorneys of "SB" objected to much of the testimony, but especially the conversation with Abbie, which they claimed would prejudice the jury. Judge Davis overruled this objection, and a number of others. Towards the end of the testimony, photographs of the murder scene were shown, much to the horror of the Fryer family.

The Log Cabin Democrat (May 22, 1915), a newspaper in nearby Conway, Arkansas, reported extensively on the trial. Its reporter wrote pages of prose about the event. One such report stated that "SB" was unmoved and not once "as witness after witness had described in minute detail the circumstances of the tragedy has Bell displayed the faintest flicker of interest. His coolness is superhuman and indeed seems to be not only mental, hut physical. While the coatless jurors perspired in the jury box, the prisoner, though clad in heavy serge, exhibited no signs of discomfort, and on one or two occasions refused fans proffered him."

It seemed that more court time and witnesses involved the sanity of "SB" than anything else, likely because "SB" had confessed that he did the killing. The defense attorneys stated often that "SB" was mentally unbalanced, that he had hallucinations, that he seemed to get lost easily, and that he had delusions of persecution. The defense witnesses spoke about changes in the behavior of "SB" after his divorce. The second day of the trial primarily involved the testimony of various physicians about the possible insanity, or at least the paranoia, of "SB". The defense brought forward four doctors, including Dr. Charles Arkebauer of the Arkansas State Hospital for Nervous Diseases, who stated that he couldn't declare "SB" insane without a thorough examination. Two other doctors who testified for the defense also agreed that while the actions of "SB" were unusual, they couldn't declare him to be insane. Only the fourth doctor would actually commit to a diagnosis of insanity. It is interesting that none of these doctors had actually interviewed or examined "SB" but were making their diagnosis based upon defense materials and what they heard at the trial.

This testimony was followed by more friends and relatives who testified that "SB" just wasn't acting normally, and his sorrow about the divorce had affected his mind. It was also stated that "SB" objected to the use of the insanity plea. Despite these witnesses, the sanity of "SB" seemed to have been determined by the testimony of Mrs. Mary Raymer, the last person to have seen him before the shootings. "SB" had stopped to visit with her about buying some cattle, and she described him as being in a "perfectly even frame of mind."

According to the law, every person was determined to be sane, even with actions and beliefs that appeared to be strange to some others. As the definition applied to crimes, there were three conditions where "SB" could be declared insane.

First, "that at the time of the killing the defendant was under such a defect of reason from disease of the mind as not to know the nature and quality of the act he was doing." Clearly, "SB" knew that he had killed people as he was able to describe his actions to a number of people during and after the shootings, so this definition did not apply.

Second, "if he did know it, that he did not know that he was doing what was wrong." Clearly, "SB" knew that what he had done was wrong as he asked about being electrocuted for his crime, so this definition did not apply.

Third, "if he knew the nature and quality of the act, and knew that it was wrong, that he was under such duress of mental disease as to be incapable of choosing between right and wrong as to the act done, and unable, because of the disease, to resist the doing of the wrong act which act was the result solely of his mental disease." This was the basis of the defense's claim of insanity. They argued that "SB" just couldn't help himself due to the stress he was under. However, the prosecution argued that this was a well-planned assault, something that required a clear mind. It was also brought up that he had conducted other activities that day in a reasonable manner. This simple idea seemed to have won the jury over.

Furthermore, crimes committed due to anger, jealousy, passion, or other emotions were not considered to be caused by insanity. Since many statements were made that the problems of "SB" were caused by his passion for his wife, some of the witnesses for the defense seemed to have actually hurt the insanity case.

Before the case went to the jury, the defense changed some of its strategy and began to plead for mercy, asking the jury to not let "SB" commit legal suicide. What was described as one of the most important parts of the trial was the closing summation by Ed Gordon. He described his earlier friendship with "SB", once a schoolmate, but how he had to now denounce him for his cruelty and brutality in killing another boyhood friend.

The testimony and attorney statements ended and the case went to the jury at 11pm after a second long day. At 12:30am on Sunday, May 23rd, the jury returned a verdict of murder in the first degree for this killing, with a recommended sentence of life imprisonment. With the verdict, Circuit Judge Marcellus L. Davis sentenced "SB" to life imprisonment in prison. A reporter wrote that Bell's face brightened when he heard the guilty verdict, but when the life in prison sentence was given, "an expression of hopelessness crept into his countenance, and he shook his head with every appearance of genuine regret."

The timing of the verdict allowed many of the Sunday papers to carry the story. Besides the bloody murders, the verdict was unusual, making for great news. This trial was the first under a new Arkansas statue which provided life imprisonment instead of execution as an option in murder cases. Because of this, the trial is often cited in legal texts across the country.

Immediately after the verdict and sentence were announced, the defense attorneys stated that there would be no appeal. However, Prosecuting Attorney Hayes stated that "SB" would be tried again, this time for the murder of Mrs. Eard Bearden. It was stated that the prosecutor was disappointed by the life sentence and that a death penalty was more appropriate. It was felt that "the details of the killing of Mrs. Bearden are much more brutal and ghastly than those of the killing of her husband."

The prosecution was reportedly not the only group disappointed with the verdict. While the family members of "SB" appeared to be relieved by the sentence of life imprisonment, Bell stated that he wished that the jury had sentenced him to the electric chair. As stated in the headlines of the *Arkansas Gazette* (May 23, 1915), "His Life is Saved, Bell Disappointed."

For the Fryer family and the local residents of Solgohachia, opinions were mixed. Many wanted revenge and justice for the dead, and the legal execution of "SB" was their goal. Others, including John Will Bearden, stated that they didn't care as long as "SB" never got out to hurt or kill anyone else. Unfortunately, neither happened.

Maye Fryer Speaks Out

Members of the Fryer family never provided testimony during the trial, but they were there. The family generally sat together supporting their mother Theresa, who seemed to be in shock much of the time. Members of the Bearden family also sat with the Fryers. Apparently, there were plans to have some members of the family testify, including Maye and Roy, but none took the witness stand. The only questions any of the Fryer family were asked was when Maye Fryer was simply asked to identify a letter sent to her by "SB".

While not providing testimony, Maye certainly was involved with the trial. She worked with the prosecuting attorneys before the trial, and often sat with them during the trial. She spent the rest of the time with her mother, as well as the mother of Erdie. Reports were that she held herself together well, crying only a few times, especially during the testimony about Bell stomping on the face of her sister and during the admission of Bell's shotgun as evidence.

It was obvious that some of the reporters needed a roster for the trial, as they seemed to have misidentified many of those who attended. Several newspapers reported that "Bell's sisters were seated near his lawyers today, as well as his former wife, Mrs. Maye Fryer." This reporting resulted in a series of letters from Maye, demanding a correction. One was printed on the front page of the May 30, 1915, edition of the *Arkansas Gazette*.

The Solgohachia Murders

> *I wish to correct a false statement of May 22. It is said that I took a seat beside my former husband's lawyers in the courtroom at Morrilton. This was untrue. I sat between Mrs. J. W. Bearden and my mother whose health has broken from grief in the loss of her husband, her son, her daughter, and her son-in-law. I was trying to console them while tears were streaming down their cheeks while witnesses were telling of my former husband's deeds of blood.*
>
> *I am not in any sympathy with him, because he never loved me. I tried to live with him and did so until I was forced to leave because of his cruel treatment. I had to go under the care of a physician to restore my health. It was his intention to murder me because he loved another woman. He often told me he loved someone else.*
>
> *My former husband was a man of intelligence, but was of a cruel disposition. His hatred for my people I trust will be developed in the next trial. I wanted to testify against him but was taken off the stand. I wish the world could know the truth, and the falsity of the rumors in regard to my attitude would be brought to a close.*
>
> *Only my husband's death in the electric chair will end the fear of our lives. I trust the citizens of this country will uphold the standard of the law which respects human blood and give to my husband death, which he most dreads.*

This would not be the last time that Maye would speak out in the family's defense, or to challenge the reporting about the murders. She spent almost the next decade having to correct stories and make statements about the activities of "SB" and their impact upon her family. I always remember her as kind and soft spoken, but apparently she was as strong-willed as anyone in the family.

The Murder Trial for the Death of Mrs. Abbie Bearden

As had been announced, a second trial was held a week later for the killing of Mrs. Abbie Bearden. Starting on Tuesday, June 1st, a new team of prosecutors and defense attorneys began to battle. The original defense attorneys, J. A. Eades of Morrilton and J. M. Henson of Leslie, added help from C. C. Reid of Little Rock, and the Morrilton law firm of Sellers & Sellers. Likewise, the prosecution gained additional staff. They include Prosecuting Attorney A. S. Hayes, Assistant Prosecuting Attorney Virgil Jordan of Morrilton, W. P. Strait of Morrilton, and Edward Gordon of Solgohachia.

The entire day involved the defense attorneys trying to squash the remaining indictments since "SB" had already been convicted of one case of murder, and claiming that the court had been illegally called. Both were overruled by Judge Marcellus L. Davis. A third challenge asked that the trial be delayed to the normal October session of the court. This challenge was overruled on the morning of June 2nd, with the result that the trial could immediately begin with the selection of a jury from 81 men, which took all day. At issue was the judge's directions that anyone who had conscientious scruples against the death penalty would be barred from sitting on the jury since it was a first-degree murder case. This requirement would come up again later in the case, and was the first time it had ever been made in Arkansas due to the recently enacted law allowing the life term instead of death in such murder cases.

Unlike the first trial, this one took more than a week. The same basic evidence used in the Eard Bearden trial was used, but additional details about the death of Abbie were included. This new evidence included information about Abbie being directly shot twice, and then while still alive, having "SB" stomp on her face. Statements about "SB" making an "improper proposal" to Abbie, and him threatening to kill her entire family, even if it took twenty years, were also reinforced with new testimony. The prosecution ended its presentation about 6:30pm, and then defense attorney Henson spoke for the next hour. The defense simply responded that "SB" was insane at the time he committed the crime and that his love for Maye preyed on his mind until he could think of nothing but revenge for taking her away from him.

The defense began the next day (June 4th) to build a case for the insanity of "SB" by having friends and family members tell their stories about his unusual, and often erratic behavior. Several of these stories seemed to work against "SB" and turned the jurors against him. In particular, Reverend Edward Lewis Tiner, a brother-in-law of "SB" (husband of Sallie Mae Bell), testified that he had asked if it was true that "SB" had stamped Abbie's face while she was on the floor, dying from her gunshot wounds. He reported that "SB" said it was a lie, he had simply put his foot over her mouth to stifle her screams so he could listen for the approach of other members of the Fryer family. Tiner added that he felt that "SB" was insane because of the way he had turned on so many friends and family members, and had stated several times that he wanted to die.

The testimony of R. L. Greer was painful to Maye and her mother, who cried and turned away when the shotgun of "SB" was presented as evidence. A new witness, Reverend Tomme, talked about his sessions with "SB". He stated that he felt that "SB" was mentally unbalanced. Pulaski County jailer Clifton Evans simply added that "SB" seemed nervous a lot of the time, but seemed more calm after a meeting with Reverend Tomme.

After the court had adjourned, "SB" was returned to his cell at the Conway County jail. That evening, he had some sort of seizure or nervous attack. Dr. Adam Robert Bradley, a local physician, was called upon to treat "SB". Bradley spent more than two hours with "SB" and called the problem a nervous breakdown bordering on paralysis. He blamed the seizure on nervous tension and poor circulation, and newspapers reported that nerves of "SB" had given way at last.

"SB" was back in court the next morning, and defense evidence was presented through noon on Saturday (June 5th), when the court was adjourned until Monday. Newspaper accounts of the first part of the trial noted the comparison between "SB" being a cunning fiend or an insane slayer. With the new week, the defense continued to bring witnesses to the stand to speak of unusual statements and actions taken by "SB". The big witness on Monday was Hugh Bell, who spoke about his many conversations with "SB". During their cross examinations, the prosecutors often consulted with Maye, who reportedly sat at their table throughout much of the trial. Reports seemed to notice changes in the appearance of "SB" who was now being described as being in a worse physical shape. They also noted that the sisters of "SB" sat with the defense attorneys but rarely said anything.

These witnesses were then followed by a series of medical experts who believed that "SB" was insane to various degrees. The day ended with the testimony of Dr. Charles Arkebauer of the Arkansas State Hospital for Nervous Diseases. Most of the testimony was the defense attorneys reading medical materials about mental diseases and asking Dr. Arkebauer if he agreed. After several objections by the prosecution, they asked Dr. Arkebauer if he felt that

"SB" should be relieved of any responsibility for the shootings. This brought an objection from the defense counsel. The jury was then dismissed for the day, the courtroom closed, and Judge Davis spent much of the evening with both sets of attorneys to review some of the objections and to work on instructions to the jury.

On Tuesday, June 8th, there was more medical testimony from Dr. Arkebauer, who again stated that "SB" had problems, calling him "paranoic" with an irrational distrust or suspicion of others. When the doctor was presented with much of the evidence already presented, he stated that it neither proved or disproved insanity. The judgement of the other doctors (Dr. C. C. Clark of Morrilton and Dr. W. A. Jones of Plumerville) was based upon the cool and calculated manner in which the killings took place. One doctor simply stated that he didn't believe a sane person could commit such a crime. However, a rebuttal witness for the prosecution was Dr. Adam Robert Bradley. Dr. Bradley had actually treated "SB" earlier in the trial when he became ill. Dr. Bradley testified that he believed "SB" to be sane. Since he was the only doctor who had actually treated "SB" for anything, his opinion carried a great deal of weight.

This testimony often went late into the evening, breaking only for meals. Maye and Roy Fryer were both expected to testify as part of the rebuttal, but were reseated as it was determined that their statements would introduce new evidence instead of simply providing rebuttal information.

On Wednesday, June 9th, the lawyers took over. Ed Gordon started the prosecution's summary, followed by defense attorney Calvin Sellers. Each spoke for two hours. Virgil Jordan then spoke for the prosecution, W. M. Hansen for the defense, and then W. P. Strait again for the prosecution. A recess was finally called at 6:30pm. The trial started again at 8:30pm with more defense provided by attorneys J. P. Sellers and J. A. Eades, taking the trial late into the evening.

The Trials and Years of Frustration

It wasn't until Thursday, June 10th, that the closing arguments were completed. Defense attorney J. A. Eades completed his arguments that "SB" was insane, but also pushed the fact that the jury had the option of recommending life imprisonment instead of the death penalty.

Much of the trial could probably be represented by the statement of Prosecuting Attorney Hayes. "I have never been able to reason out why any sane man should commit a crime. But in this case, I want you to know that you are dealing with a man who is absolutely sane, a man who is reckless with the lives of others, and who is regardless of their happiness." The case went to the jury that afternoon, with members of the Fryer, Bearden and Bell families sitting in the courtroom hoping for a quick finding and sentence. Unfortunately, it didn't come, although the jury almost immediately agreed on a guilty verdict. The jury was given a break at 10pm.

The next day, the jury met with the judge twice to report that it couldn't reach a unanimous decision on the sentence. The vote was 11 for the death sentence, and 1 for the life sentence based upon a possible temporary insanity at the time of the shooting. Judge Davis declined to discharge the jury and instructed the members to continue their work. Some reports stated that the judge had possibly reminded the members of the jury that they had promised to deliver a death sentence despite any conscientious scruples against it. The jury returned on Saturday morning (June 12th) with a guilty verdict and a sentence of death.

Feelings were mixed in the courtroom. Many of those in attendance quietly celebrated, thinking that this was the end. The three sisters of "SB" (Frances, born 1873; Sallie, born 1878; and Zella, born 1895) openly wept and Hugh Bell and the defense attorneys immediately filed an appeal, plus a motion for a new trial based upon a number of claimed errors by the judge. "SB" stated that he was glad to die, and told several people this fact. It was reported that he was more cheerful than at any time during the trial.

Later that Saturday, Conway County Sheriff J. M. Gordon brought "SB" first to the Pulaski County jail, and then to the Arkansas penitentiary on Sunday, until the verdict and sentence could be officially read. On Wednesday, June 16, 1915, less than two months after the shootings, "SB" was back in the courtroom at Morrilton. There, Judge Marcellus Davis read the guilty verdict and announced the death sentence.

After reading the sentence, Judge Davis asked "SB" if he had any reason why the sentence should not be passed upon him. "SB" refused to answer the judge. Judge Davis then made what can only be described as a passionate statement as part of his ruling. "I had hoped it would not ever fall to my lot during my brief incumbency to have to perform this duty. I will not exaggerate the pain to either of us. After the long, arduous trial nothing remains to be said. It seems you are approaching the portals where all must soon pass to that mysterious world beyond the shores of time. Your spiritual welfare will be attended to by those better qualified than myself to perform that duty before your surcease of sorrow on earth."

The date of August 20, 1915, was set for his execution by electrocution. "SB" stated that he had received an easy sentence since he would rather die than serve a life sentence. However, with the completion of the second trial, "SB" and his family began their efforts to set him free despite his murder convictions.

The Arkansas Supreme Court Appeal

The appeal process began the next day, and on June 17th, Judge Davis denied the motion of a new trial. "SB" reportedly told his lawyers to halt the appeal, but Hugh

Bell continued the efforts. He had the attorneys file a suit against the State of Arkansas (*Bell v. State*) saying that "SB" couldn't be charged with the murder of Mrs. Bearden since the act was part of the same event for which he had already been convicted. The defense had already stated that "the killing of the two persons was but one transaction and constituted one offense; that the proof to sustain one would sustain the other; that his conviction of the killing of Eard Bearden was also tantamount to convicting him of the killing of Abbie Bearden. for which he was about to be tried." This argument had been thrown out, but they tried again to no avail.

On August 7, 1915, Chief Justice E. A. McCulloch of the Arkansas Supreme Court granted the appeal of "SB", acting as a stay of execution. The attorneys for "SB" had challenged the trial for additional reasons.

A challenge to the sentence of death was immediately made. The attorneys for Bell contended that the wording of the new law had abolished capital punishment, making life imprisonment the only possible punishment in such convictions. A review of the new law, Act No. 187 dated March 20, 1915, and entitled *An Act giving the jury the right to render a verdict of life imprisonment in the State penitentiary in all cases where the punishment is now death by law*, as well as a ruling by the Arkansas Supreme Court, found that the law only allowed life imprisonment as an option to the death sentence, not a requirement or a ban of the older practice. The actual statement read "That the jury shall have the right in all cases where the punishment is now death by law to render a verdict of life imprisonment in the State penitentiary at hard labor."

The defense attorneys next challenged the ruling that members of the jury could not have any conscientious scruples against the death penalty. This had been an important part of the instructions given to the jury by Judge Marcellus L. Davis, and had been used to end the 11-1 divide on the sentence for the murder conviction. The Arkansas Supreme Court concluded that "Capital punishment being the law in this State, where trial juries may return a verdict which would result in capital punishment, the State, in the trial of cases when the death penalty may be imposed, is entitled to a jury that has no conscientious scruples as to such penalty." This concept soon became the standard nationwide where capital punishment was the law.

The defense attorneys also filed a suit stating that his conviction was illegal because the Conway Circuit Court was incorrectly called. This too was thrown out, as the Arkansas Supreme Court found that a circuit judge could hold a special term of the circuit court for many reasons, including to try a person confined in jail.

Another major challenge was that "SB" was criminally insane and not responsible for his actions, and that some of the witnesses were not proper. The issue of the sanity of "SB" came up in both trials, with friends and neighbors providing examples of strange and unnatural things that he had recently done. Medical experts also questioned whether he was sane during the killings since he seemed to be cool and calm during the horrific event. It was generally stated by defense witnesses that "SB" knew that his acts were a violation of the law but still wasn't capable of making a choice between right and wrong. However, prosecution witnesses used his same cool actions to point to a group of murders that had been well-planned, something an insane person could not have done. It was determined by the Arkansas Supreme Court that when:

> *reason is temporarily dethroned, not by disease, but by anger, jealousy, or other passion; nor will he be excused because he has become so morally depraved "that his conscience ceases to control*

or influence his actions." In other words, neither so-called "emotional" nor "moral" insanity will justify or excuse a crime.

This and other parts of the conditions of insanity, established by the Arkansas Supreme Court, began to be used nationwide, another precedent established by this case.

The two convictions of murder, each with a different sentence, provided the attorneys for "SB" an opportunity, despite "SB" expressing "regret that he had not been condemned to be electrocuted" after the first trial. Just a few weeks before the murders and trials, Arkansas had changed its law on murder cases, allowing sentences of life in prison versus the older law that only allowed the death sentence for those convicted of the crime.

The new law was part of a series of changes in the Arkansas death sentence. Prior to 1913, all executions were by hanging except for four guerillas who were shot on July 29, 1864. In 1913, the method of execution was primarily changed to the electric chair, a device built from wood that had previously made up the state gallows. Another change was the centralization of executions at the State Penitentiary in Little Rock instead of in the county where the conviction took place. The requirement of execution in all murder convictions changed in 1915. The Act of 1915 read as follows: "That the jury shall have the right in all cases where the punishment is now death by law, to render a verdict of life imprisonment in the State penitentiary at hard labor." The new law did not repeal the death penalty, instead it added the option of life imprisonment.

"SB" now had conflicting sentences, and the confusion about how the law was to be applied led the Arkansas Supreme Court to state that "SB" was entitled to a new trial because of errors in instructions to the jury. However, the court also ruled that just because "SB" had been previously sentenced to life imprisonment for another murder it was not impossible that the death sentence could be imposed upon him. This issue of two conflicting sentences resulted in further hearings, and a great deal of debate, because the new Arkansas law never accounted for such a situation. The Supreme Court did state that the first sentence imposed had precedence over the second, meaning that the life imprisonment essentially had to take place before the death sentence could be enforced. This ruling established another precedent that impacted the entire United States.

The multiple court cases, as well as the numerous challenges and appeals, led to a large amount of documentation about the murders, and the events that led to them. The following are just a small part of the story found in the records of the Supreme Court of Arkansas.

> *The testimony on behalf of the State tended to show that on the 26th day of April, 1915, appellant at about 8 o'clock p.m., killed in rapid succession, with a repeating shotgun, Eard Bearden, his wife, Abbie Bearden, Dick Fryer, her father, and Amos Fryer, her brother; that several months prior to the killing appellant had insulted Mrs. Abbie Bearden; that he made indecent proposals to her; that he had used an offensive epithet towards her about which she informed her husband Eard Bearden; that the latter had appellant arrested for a breach of peace; that in consequence of such arrest appellant became deeply incensed and threatened to kill Mrs. Abbie Bearden if it took him twenty years and if he had to slip up in the night and shoot her; that he engaged in a fight with Eard Bearden, cutting him severely; that soon after this appellant's wife, who was a sister of Mrs. Abbie Bearden, secured a divorce from*

him and went to live with her own people; that appellant claimed that the separation of his wife from him was caused by Mrs. Abbie Bearden and his wife's people and his own people; that appellant believed that this separation and divorce had damaged his reputation, and that in consequence of all these things appellant was mad with Mrs. Bearden and her husband and the others whom he slew; that his ill will continued on to the time of the homicides, and that he made threats to kill them; that he armed himself and sought out the persons whom he killed and slew them with malice aforethought and in a spirit of revenge growing out of the previous trouble which appellant claimed those persons had caused him.

The appellant did not deny the killing. A plea of insanity was interposed in his behalf, and evidence was adduced by him tending to show that up to the time of the trouble with Mrs. Bearden and her husband he had borne a good reputation in the community where he lived; that his wife was a young lady of irreproachable character, to whom he was devotedly attached; that his love and devotion continued, nothwithstanding the divorce, to the time of the killing; that soon after his marriage, without any apparent reason or just cause, he conceived the idea that his wife's relatives and his own relatives were trying to cause him and his wife to separate; that it was through their influence that the separation and divorce were brought about; that when brooding over his family troubles he would express intense love and devotion for his wife, and on these occasions would break down and shed tears, stating

> *that he regarded himself as ruined, that his life was worth nothing to him that he would as soon be dead as alive; that this condition of his mind gradually grew worse; that he lost his appetite, lost flesh, was unable to sleep, would lie in bed and groan and grit his teeth for practically the entire night; that he censured his own sister, who had raised him, accusing her of being a bitter enemy against him in his troubles, saying that he didn't have any more use for her than he did for a yellow negro; that before this time he had always spoken of her in terms of the tenderest affection; that he likewise censured his own brother, stating that his brother had accused him of being crazy; also he had censured his uncle with both of these before that time he had been on affectionate terms; that he threatened to kill his own people and his wife's people, accusing them all of having turned against him and having ruined his life, saying that they had gotten everybody down on him, and that when he passed his acquaintances he imagined they were saying "there goes that damned crazy son of a bitch;" that notwithstanding his uncle's persistent denials that he had anything against him he continued still to angrily accuse him.*

Eventually, the Supreme Court of Arkansas ruled on all of the details of the appeal on November 8, 1915. Its ruling included two important findings that were cited for years in various legal cases.

> (1) The conviction of defendant for the murder of A. would not be a bar to his trial and conviction for the murder of B., when the killings were not simultane-

ous, nor the result of one shot, but were the results of entirely separate acts.

(2) The fact that appellant was convicted and was then undergoing life imprisonment for the murder of A. would not preclude his being tried and, after verdict, suffering the death penalty for the murder of B.

However, the death sentence for murder was reversed by the Arkansas Supreme Court on November 8th, due to errors in the instructions of the court to the jury. As stated by the court, technical errors in instructions submitted to the jury by Judge M. L. Davis prejudiced the convicted man's case. By this time, "SB" was already in the state penitentiary, where he had arrived on May 20, 1915. Since he had two commitment papers – one for the death penalty and one for a life imprisonment – he was treated based upon the most severe penalty. He was to be electrocuted on August 20th, so he was not forced to work or wear the striped clothing of a convict.

An article in the *Boston Evening Globe* (July 27, 1915), and carried in other newspapers, reported on the legal issues created by the two separate trials. It was stated that the life sentence was "a bar to the death sentence unless the Governor first pardons him in the life term." It became more complicated because a pardoned prisoner had to accept a pardon. Because of this, officers stated that "SB" could not be executed under the death sentence, nor could he be sent to the State Convict Farm under the life sentence, because he was supposed to occupy the death cell. Eventually, "SB" was treated as a common criminal and was forced to wear the uniform of a convict and to work at the prison.

The Solgohachia Murders

The Penitentiary, Escape, and a Furlough

The various appeals delayed the execution, and then it was overturned, forcing "SB" to begin working in the prison fields and shops. In early November, it was announced that "SB" would not be tried at a special term of court at Morrilton on account of the unusual expense it would require (reportedly $4,096.35 had already been spent by the county). Instead, he would get another hearing during the regular term in March 1916. Meanwhile, he was serving a life term in the penitentiary for the first murder. By January 1916, "SB" was at the State Convict Farm at Cummins, where he made news by not being part of a large escape from the stockade at the farm. In March, three charges of murder still existed against "SB" and there was debate on whether trials would ever be held. Things seemed to have quieted down on the case, but this lasted only a few years.

On Friday, October 31, 1919, "SB" was part of a gang of convicts from the State Convict Farm at Tucker who were delivering wheat to a mill in Pine Bluff. During this trip, "SB" complained of a bad tooth and was taken to a dentist. The tooth was apparently a major project, and the dentist instructed him to return on Saturday to complete the work. The prison's warden approved the visit and didn't require an escort. "SB" hadn't returned by the following Monday afternoon, and newspaper accounts stated that the warden finally determined that "SB" had left Pine Bluff without notifying farm officials of his destination. As the *Pine Bluff Daily Graphic* reported in their November 5, 1919, edition, Sam Bell quit the penal farm. In other words, he had escaped and fled the area. A reward was immediately posted for his recapture.

The subject of the location of "SB" came up now and then, and there were reports of strangers who would stalk members of the Fryer family and their friends. Family legend states that members of the Fryer family were constantly on the lookout for "SB". Eventually he was found on a dairy farm outside Dallas on April 18, 1922. At first "SB" denied that he was an escaped convict and claimed to be Joe Smith (some sources state John Smith). He had even married a woman who was the niece of a Dallas Patrolman. She also kept claiming his innocence. The performance ended when Sheriff R. E. Bartlett of Morrilton arrived and identified "SB" as the wanted convict. "SB" actually shook the hand of Sheriff Bartlett, saying "Well, Sheriff, I guess you got me again."

The capture was reported by the Associated Press and the news was sent across the country. Numerous newspapers reported on the capture, and many had some small errors in the reporting. For example, *The Brownsville Herald* of Brownsville, Texas, stated that "Bell is charged with killing his wife, his brother-in-law and two other men in Plummerville." It did add some details about where "SB" had been hiding when it reported that "he had been here [Dallas] about six months. Previously he had worked in the oil fields." *The Birmingham Age-Herald* included in their reporting that when "he married the second time he told his wife about his previous trouble, but they agreed they would try to forget it."

The German language newspaper *Arkansas Echo*, published in Little Rock, had one of the better articles about Bell's capture in their April 27, 1922, edition.

> *In Dallas, Texas, Sam Bell, who escaped from the penitentiary, has been found and brought back. Six years ago, Bell had beaten his wife and shot four of her relatives to death at Solgohatchia and was sentenced to life in prison. Two years ago, he escaped and came to Dallas, where he obtained work as a milkman under the name John*

> Smith. There he worked skillfully and reliably, and was accepted as a partner in the business, and John Smith married. The Express Company that he did business with sent him a questionnaire to fill out. John Smith left unanswered the questions as to where he came from and what he had done before. The express company and the sheriff sought the answers and found them. John Smith was returned to the penitentiary here as Sam Bell.

Reports from the Arkansas penitentiary system indicate that there had been fear that "SB" would attempt an escape, so he had been made a "trusty" and moved to the Cummins prison farm which was used primarily for black prisoners. Here it was considered to be easier to track his movements. However, based upon the many news articles about the escape and recapture of "SB" it is obvious that he had received large sums of money shortly before his escape. When he went to Pine Bluff, he bought a ticket on the St. Louis Southwestern Railway to the Dallas area. He found work in the oil fields at Ranger, Texas, but was injured in about a year. He then worked dressing tools before applying for work with the American Railway Express Agency, which had been created by the United States Railroad Administration in 1918. As part of his application, a photo was taken of "SB" and he was asked to fill out a job application that included information about his background. His failure to answer certain questions led the firm to have the Pinkerton detectives conduct a background search on him.

Meanwhile, an office job was available at the Dallas office of the American Railway Express Agency and he was temporarily hired. After only five months, "SB" quit the job and began working in the local dairy industry. He also married a girl from Mineral Wells in 1921. In September

The Trials and Years of Frustration

1921, "SB" acquired half-interest in a dairy farm located between Dallas and Vickery, where he was arrested after the Pinkerton's and local law enforcement had determined his true identify.

Sheriff Bartlett returned "SB" to the Arkansas penitentiary, and in 1924 "SB" returned to a court at Morrilton where he pled guilty to the remaining two indictments and was given two additional life sentences. At the same time the death penalty was commuted to life imprisonment, which left Bell serving four life terms. During the early 1920s, Thomas Chipman McRae served as the 26th Governor of Arkansas. Before he stepped down after his second term on January 13, 1925, McRae received a letter requesting he act on the sentences of "SB" and his request for a pardon. As stated in several newspapers, the governor refused to extend clemency to Sam Bell of Conway County, "who was convicted in April for the murder of four of his wife's relatives at Solgohachia in 1915."

In the 1930 census, "SB" was shown to be an inmate in the Arkansas State Convict Farm No. 1 in Dudley Lake, Jefferson County. However, "SB" wasn't there much longer as in December, Arkansas Governor Parnell issued a six-month furlough to "SB". In April 1931, Parnell indefinitely extended the furlough, and the hell of Sam Bell returned to the Fryer family and their friends and neighbors.

It should be noted that Governor Parnell furloughed a number of killers, at least one of which was convicted of killing several law officers both before and after the furlough. There are few known direct ties between "SB" and Governor Harvey Parnell, but both were in the cattle business and Parnell was a political progressive known for his strong use of local party bosses, county patronage rolls, and friends and acquaintances to get his way. What was known as the "Parnell Machine" was charged with campaign finance irregularities, and was accused of running an ineffective administration, if not one that was outright corrupt. During the late 1920s, Parnell pushed through numerous spending bills and new taxes, and then quickly spent the state's share of relief from the resources of the Reconstruction Finance Corporation and the Red Cross. There were reports that he was looking for ways to reduce spending and to raise funds by the early 1930s, but no clear connection between the two individuals has been found. After serving as governor since 1928, Parnell retired in 1933.

Parnell's actions certainly hurt the Fryer family. "SB" apparently moved to Texas and then back to Plumerville, Arkansas, and for the next several decades he would show up at Fryer family homes and businesses, and there were numerous reports that he would approach friends of the family and simply ask them if they knew the Fryers. My grandmother reported that "SB" would stand outside their home under a streetlight, looking up at the house. He also used to park his car across the street from the home of Aunt Toots (Maye) and sit in the car. While he never directly attacked the family, he did become an evil ghost for them for years, and many stated that they felt like they were being stalked. Any family gathering was accompanied by the fear that "SB" would show up with his shotgun.

Other families also reported strange appearances of "SB", or changed their habits to protect themselves from him. For example, during the 1930s, Wilma Aleta (Miller) Tarpley reported that "SB" appeared at the Hope (Arkansas) hotel operated by her and her husband. Members of the Miller family had been friends of the Fryers and had helped the family after the shootings of 1915. While no threats were made, the word was apparently passed on that "SB" was traveling from Texas to Plumerville. Family stories also state that members of the Gordon family pulled their curtains closed before dinner so that they were not clearly visible from outside the house while eating.

The Trials and Years of Frustration

During the late 1930s and early 1940s, many of the Fryer brothers and sisters settled on Park Hill in North Little Rock, Arkansas. At the time, this was a new development with clean well water, paved streets, and a slightly cooler environment due to the elevation and breezes. About Christmas in 1939, T. B. and Gladys Wilson moved into a house at 301 West F Street. Clay and Maye Sisemore soon moved into a nearby house at 329 West G Street. William "Buddy" Fryer also acquired a house, this one at 617 West D Street. Bernice and Bob Finnegan bought a home next door to Buddy at 619 West D Street. This grouping of Fryer homes provided a support system, especially during the regular visits by "SB".

This house on West F Street on Park Hill was the home of my grandmother for most of her life. Photo by Barton Jennings.

This well-kept house, located on West G Street, was the home of Maye and Clay Sisemore for about twenty-five years. Photo by Barton Jennings.

The Final Bell Trials

The family fear of possible violence was certainly valid, as on November 14, 1961, "SB" shot and wounded his own nephew, William Robert (Billy Bob) Bell, a former Marine Sergeant who had fought in World War II and Korea. Billy Bob was the son of Ed M. Bell, the youngest brother of "SB". "SB's" youngest sister, Mrs. Lu Zella Bell Loney, died in 1961 and left her estate to two of her nephews. "SB" and his brother Joe Bell protested the will, stating that Lu Zella wasn't in her right mind when the will was written in 1956. On November 14th, William Bell and his mother were heading to a hearing on the will. Leaving Plumerville, they were attacked by "SB", who had been hiding in some bushes about 20 yards away. He fired two shots with his shotgun, wounding Billy Bob Bell in the hand and leg.

"SB" fled the scene after Billy Bob returned fire with his own gun, and hid from law officials for a short period of time. He eventually turned himself in to W. O. Hice, the Conway County tax assessor located in the courthouse at Morrilton. As part of the planning for a trial, "SB" was examined at the Arkansas State Hospital. Doctors there ruled that "SB" was probably not responsible for his actions, but "SB" demanded a hearing in circuit court. In February 1962, "SB" was found guilty (some sources state that he pled guilty) on a charge of assault with intent to kill and was sentenced to fifteen years imprisonment. By this time, the syphilis that he had carried for almost fifty years caught up with him, and he died from the disease in the penitentiary on November 28, 1962. With his burial in the Plumerville Cemetery, much of the fear in the Fryer family eroded away. However, the years of pain and the efforts to forget the horrors that "SB" had imposed on the family more than 47 years earlier kept the matter a secret to many, with members of the family taking their stories to their graves.

It is interesting though that the death of "SB" didn't end the horrors for his own family. William Robert Bell sued "SB" for $121,000 to cover damages from the shooting, but "SB" died before the case was heard. Meanwhile, "SB" had given his possessions and wealth to his favorite niece, and his truck to another nephew. After the funeral expenses were paid, the money was passed on to a daughter who gave half to Kenneth Coffelt, the attorney who had represented "SB" and his niece, as part of a plan to build a hotel. This action led to a series of lawsuits between family members. The courts actually took possession of the funds for some time, awaiting a final opinion on the matter.

The primary legal case was *Dereuisseaux v. Bell*, with an opinion delivered on May 4, 1964, by the Arkansas Supreme Court. The court ruled that "SB" did not have the right to give away his property. The case provided additional information about the shooting and the financial manipulations involved. When the 1961 shooting took place, "SB" was living near Lake Conway and owned real and personal property worth about $25,000. Between January and May, 1962, "SB" transferred all of his property and wealth to Leila Dereuisseaux (except a truck given to a nephew). It was determined that the exchange was executed with the fraudulent intention of placing the property of "SB" beyond the reach of William Robert Bell. The ruling even covered the issue that those who accepted the funds, including the attorney Kenneth Coffelt, could not be considered innocent recipients of the assets. Recollecting these funds took several more court cases and several more years.

"The evil that men do lives after them."

The Unknown Trial

In the midst of the series of murder trials, there was another arrest and trial that has always been overlooked. Following the murders, the Fryer homes mainly sat empty. Some basic repairs were made to the home of Erdie and Abbie to seal it, and the home of Dick Fryer was locked up. However, on July 15, 1915, Mun Robinson was arrested for stealing about $20 worth of clothes and household goods from "the home of the late Eard Bearden." At his arrest, Robinson was even found to be wearing a hat that belonged to Eard.

There are few reports about the arrest and trial, but Robinson was apparently sentenced to several years in prison, and was made a trusty guard at the Tucker Convict Farm. On July 6, 1917, he was part of a posse that was attempting to capture six escapees, including Carl Vogan, who had shot several people during a bank robbery. Vogan was killed and the other five escapees were recaptured. Mun Robinson was seriously wounded during the pursuit.

The Fryer Family Post-1915

The Fryer family was a typically large one for the time and many members survived the murders of April 26th. However, as a family member once wrote, "S. Bell lived forever afterwards" and "the sucker laid a dark shadow over the whole family for years and years."

The events on April 26th impacted the Fryer family for the rest of their lives. Few ever spoke of the event and many moved away and would never return to the old farm. Several members of the family never recovered, taking up drinking and/or acting strangely at certain times or in response to certain sounds. There were family reunions, even at the Fryer farm, some of which I remember. However, any mention of the shooting quickly broke up the gatherings, and I never got the details first-hand.

The survivors of the shooting lived varied lives. Some started successful businesses while others held positions at well-known companies. Others became known in the sporting world or the military. Their descendants had similar stories, and have spread across the country. This chapter is designed to cover the history of the survivors, and show what could have become of the victims if there was no Bell shooting.

The Fryer Family Moves Away

After the shootings on the Fryer Farm near Solgohachia, few of those who had lived there spent much time on the property. Porter Henry was already living at his own place with his wife, Laura, but most of the rest of the survivors moved to a large house in Morrilton, with a few rooms rented out as a boarding house. By 1920, Theresa Fryer and many of her children had moved to Little Rock where she operated a large boarding house. Many of the children married and lived in the Little Rock area, while one returned to Morrilton and several others lived around the United States.

While of poor quality, this is one of the few photographs of the Fryer family living in Morrilton. The back row features Theresa, Gladys and Buddy, while on the front row is Dwight, Elmo and Bernice. Photo from the collection of Tomme Jennings.

The Fryer Farm, however, wasn't abandoned or immediately sold. Instead, James P. Fryer (Uncle Jim), the brother of Richard Thomas "Dick" Fryer, lived on his adjacent property and worked the farm of Dick Fryer for years. James P. Fryer (1863-1934) married Mollie Holder (1869-1919), and they had five children, four who were alive when the shooting occurred. Annie Fryer (1895-1949) was the oldest child and married Joe H. Merrick in 1921. She ran the

The Fryer Family Post-1915

mail route for a number of years, ending in February 1943. Ollie Allen Fryer (1897-1969) was the oldest son and he worked the farm with his father. After the death of James P. Fryer, Ollie took over operating the entire farm complex. He was known for his two mules which were almost part of the family. He had them properly buried when they died. Nettie Faye Fryer (1900-1959) was the next oldest and lived much of her life on the family farm. Ruby Fryer Benton (1904-1979) was the youngest daughter. She married Harlen V. Benton. The last child, James Fuller Fryer, was born on February 8, 1908, and died on April 13, 1908. All lived their entire lives in the area and were buried in the Solgohachia Friendship Cemetery.

James P. Fryer and his family worked Dick's farm after his death. Photo from the collection of Tomme Jennings.

The Solgohachia Murders

For more than 80 years, the survivors of the shootings lived with the memories of April 26, 1915. Their histories, and the histories of their immediate children, are told here.

Some photos just had to be used in this book. Here, Bart Wilson and Elmo Fryer show off their style, very reminiscent of the classic gangster movies of the 1930s and 1940s. Photo from the collection of Tomme Jennings.

Theresa Reiter Fryer (1868-1956)

Theresa Reiter was the wife of Richard Thomas "Dick" Fryer, head of the Fryer family at the time of the shooting and one of the victims. Theresa was born on October 12, 1868, in Austria. The Reiter family was from Grossarl, Austria, a mountain village south of Salzburg that is now considered to be a resort destination. At the time, Grossarl was part of the Austro-Hungarian Monarchy (separate parliaments in Austria and Hungary with an emperor ruling over the empire), which saw a massive migration to the United States by 1880. Many were farmers who were seeing fields being replaced by industry and new cities. This economic change created a large disparity between the developing regions of Austria-Hungary and the farming areas. About the same time, the government was also using conscription to rebuild its military after a series of defeats. Taking advantage of this, American railroads had immigration agents in the area selling farm land that had been acquired as land grants. The land also generally included the transportation required to move the family, and sometimes temporary jobs building or maintaining the railroad.

In 1880, the Reitter family (Johann, Barbara, two girls and five boys) left Grossarl and emigrated to the United States. They arrived at Baltimore, Maryland, on December 16, 1880, and took a train to Conway County, Arkansas. The entire trip was apparently part of a purchase of land in the Arkansas River Valley, likely from the Little Rock & Fort Smith Railway, which sold thousands of acres of land grant properties to German immigrants. Johann "John" Reiter (1832-1923) and his wife Barbara Weber Reiter (1841-1908) arrived at Morrilton and settled in the area, with Saint Vincent often mentioned. With them was their daughter Theresa "Thresa" Reiter. The arrival of many Roman Catholics from Germany and Austria created some conflicts in the area, as most of the earlier settlers followed various Protestant faiths, especially Methodism. This hard feeling was apparently especially true between the Methodist Fryer and Catholic Reiter families.

After the family's arrival in Arkansas, Theresa and Richard apparently had seen each other several times despite the conflict between the Catholic and Methodist families and religions. One day while neighbors had gathered to harvest crops, Theresa was being picked on by others. Richard stepped up to defend her and ended the name calling. After a courtship that was disapproved of by both families, Dick and Theresa married on October 14, 1888. They moved to the Fryer farm near Solgohachia and eventually occupied the main house.

The night of the shooting, Theresa apparently organized the family inside the house while Dick confronted Sam Bell. She directed much of the family to hide in nearby fields before heading out the front of the house to find out what had happened to her husband and son Amos. It is likely that she too would have been shot and killed if several sons hadn't pulled her away from the scene. She, and much of the family, fled to the safety of the homes of neighbors.

After the shooting and trial, Theresa (generally spelled Thresa by the family and called Mammaw by many) reportedly took to her bed and remained nonfunctional for a year or more. According to family legend, one day the family doctor came to see Theresa and told her he wanted her to sell everything in Solgohachia, move the family somewhere else, and never talk about the killings again. Theresa and much of her family had remained in the Morrilton area during the trial, and then ran a boarding house there. To make space for roomers, all of the boys reportedly slept on a balcony over the front porch. This also gave them views of the surrounding neighborhood.

The Fryer Family Post-1915

By the 1920 census (January 27, 1920), the family had moved to Little Rock. There, Mrs. Fryer bought a boarding house at 220 Broadway in Little Rock, one that was soon known for the fine meals that were served. Later, Theresa Fryer moved to a new boarding house just two blocks away at 608 West Third in Little Rock, now a parking lot. The two boarding houses both started as large private homes, built by the early 1900s. After Theresa Fryer moved, the Broadway house was replaced by a used car lot. The Third Street house was brick with a slate roof, and was shown to be 2½ stories tall. For years, the attic was used by male students at a local barber school who came with references, basically a bunk house with beds and chest of drawers. The second floor had 8 to 10 rooms that were rented to "nice ladies." A few rooms were used by members of the Fryer family, especially during the years of the Great Depression.

Theresa Reiter Fryer, known as Mammaw by many in the family, had her health almost destroyed by the shooting. While she ran boarding houses almost until the time of her death, she heavily relied upon her children and hired help. Photo from the collection of Tomme Jennings.

As stated, the children of Mammaw Fryer often assisted her in operating the boarding houses, and also often took her to their various farms and homes. This picture shows Mammaw with Maye, plus Laura, the wife of Porter. Photo from the collection of Tomme Jennings.

This is a photo of Mammaw (Theresa Reiter Fryer) during her later years while operating a boarding house in Little Rock, Arkansas. Photo from the collection of Tomme Jennings.

There were also several small buildings in the backyard, shown as 608-1/2 (1 story) and 608-1/3 (a garage with a room above). These were shown to be servant quarters when the house was a private residence, and later used as residence space with the cook living over the garage. The cook, a black women named Sadie, worked for Theresa for many years before moving to California about the time the boarding house closed. Besides those who rented a room, the boarding house also served meals to a number of local businessmen, leading to several marriages. Theresa's children helped to operate the boarding house, but Theresa later hired help due to her frail health. During the last years of her boarding house, Theresa generally handled the paperwork and paid others to do the manual work.

It is interesting that the street addresses of the boarding houses, and many of the personal houses of the Fryer family, are still remembered. The reason has a fascinating explanation. Family members almost never said the names of the people at their destination, but would instead state the address where they were heading. Therefore, those heading to see Theresa at the boarding house would simply report that they were heading to 608 West Third. Apparently, another small part of the paranoia created by the shootings.

For years, Theresa remained vigilant as Sam Bell either escaped or was released from prison. During this time, she reported numerous occasions of strange cars parked outside her house, and of Sam Bell standing under a nearby streetlight staring at the house. During the last few years of her life, Theresa had several strokes and was ill, generally bedridden or confined to a wheelchair. Because of this, she was living with Clay and Maye Sisemore (Uncle Si and Aunt Toots). After one of her last strokes, she could only speak German and a local priest in North Little Rock would come out and talk with her.

The Solgohachia Murders

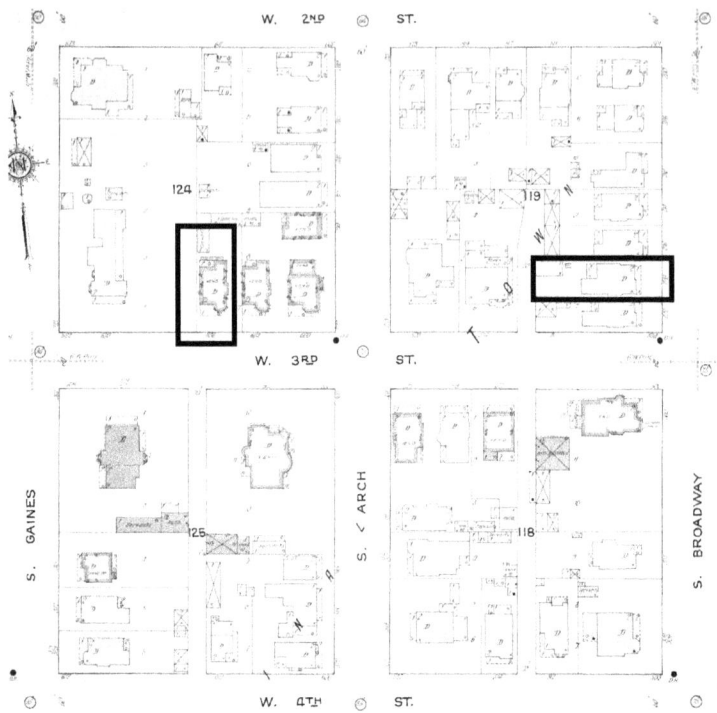

This map of Little Rock from 1913 shows the two houses – 220 Broadway and 608 West Third – that were later used by Theresa Reiter Fryer as boarding houses. *Sanborn Fire Insurance Map from Little Rock, Pulaski County, Arkansas.* Sanborn Map Company, Vol.1, 1913. Map. Retrieved from the Library of Congress, https://www.loc.gov/item/sanborn00285_005/.

Theresa Reiter Fryer passed away at Little Rock on August 17, 1956, at the age of 87. She was buried at Roselawn Memorial Park in Little Rock. Until the end, Sam Bell formed a dark cloud over her head as family members were certain that the murderer would appear at the funeral.

The Fryer Family Post-1915

This stone marks the final resting place of Thresa Reiter Fryer, located in Roselawn Memorial Park in Little Rock, Arkansas. Photo by Barton Jennings.

Len Reiter was the older brother of Theresa Reiter Fryer, and he sometimes worked on the Fryer farm. He was the only Reiter to be buried in the Solgohachia Friendship Community Cemetery, and his grave is surrounded by graves of various members of the Fryer family. Photo by Barton Jennings

Roy Thomas Fryer (1890-1962)

Roy Thomas Fryer, known by many as Roy or Uncle Roy, was the second child from the Richard-Theresa marriage. The first child died at birth on July 9, 1889, and Roy was born almost a year later on June 28, 1890. Being the oldest son, Roy often worked and traveled with his father, Dick. As the trouble began between the Fryers and Bell, Roy was one of the family members threatened during several of Bell's visits to Solgohachia. During early 1914, Bell had attacked Roy just several hours before he pulled a blade on Erdie.

Apparently, Roy was at the main house, or arrived there as the shooting began. While the name Lloyd was used in several newspaper articles, it was stated that the eldest son helped to carry Theresa Fryer away from the scene. However, his name was seldom mentioned in the trials that followed, except for statements that there was trouble between Bell and Roy Fryer. Apparently, while there were plans by the prosecution to have Roy testify at the murder trials as part of the rebuttal efforts, the court did not allow it as it was determined that his statements would introduce new evidence instead of simply providing rebuttal information.

The Garrett family, Wiley W. and Millie E. Garrett, lived to the northeast of Solgohachia near the communities of Birdtown and Cypress Valley. They had four daughters, and on September 8, 1917, Roy married Vickie (Victoria) Agnes Garrett (1894-1978) in Conway County. Roy Thomas Fryer worked for the Coca-Cola Bottling Company of Morrilton, where he later retired. He then moved to Little Rock where he passed away on October 9, 1962. He was buried in Elmwood Cemetery at Morrilton, where his wife Vickie Agnes was buried when she died in 1978.

On June 1, 1918, their son Jack Thomas Fryer (1918-2009) was born at Morrilton, Arkansas. Jack Tom, as he was known, played varsity football and basketball at Morrilton High School and Hendrix College, and then served in the Air Force during World War II, being awarded the Air Medal with three Oak Leaf Clusters and the Distinguished Flying Cross. Jack Tom was noted as being a lucky pilot, and everyone wanted to fly with him. Three times he was so late returning that others had already divided up his belongings and he had to go get them back. He later worked in the furniture business, owning Jack T. Fryer Furniture and then becoming a manufacturer's representative for several furniture companies. Jack Tom met Alice Camille Bishop when she moved to Little Rock to work for the U.S. Agricultural Department. Known as "Big Al" by many, Alice started playing golf in her 50s and soon won a number of tournaments around Arkansas and the south. In 1996, she became part of the third class of the Arkansas Golf Hall of Fame.

A daughter, Barbara Faye Fryer, was born to Roy and Vickie on January 25, 1920. Barbara worked as a teacher, and then built fuses for bombs at the Jacksonville Ordinance Arsenal during World War II. For several years, she lived at the Little Rock boarding house of Theresa Fryer. She lived in the back of the house and had her own bathroom not used by other boarders. On August 23, 1950, Barbara married Herschel Samuel Davis, and together they owned Davis Rubber Company, often claimed to be the world's oldest tire recycling company. They also owned Davis Ranch, several thousand acres of cattle ranch north of Gravel Ridge, Arkansas. I knew the ranch well as I camped there a number of times, generally without understanding the family connections. On January 6, 2023, less than three weeks from her 103rd birthday, Barbara Faye passed away, having checked herself out of a hospital a year earlier.

Another son, Donnie Kenneth Fryer (1938-2006), was born on December 22, 1938.

Don married Rose Dyles on January 12, 1962, and was the owner of CISCO Enterprises Inc. He passed away in Conway, and was then buried in Morrilton in Elmwood Cemetery, just a few feet from his father.

The grave of Roy T. and Vickie A. Fryer can be found in Elmwood Cemetery in Morrilton, Arkansas, just a short distance from Solgohachia. Photo by Barton Jennings.

Porter Henry Fryer (1894-1973)

Porter, often called Rock, was my Uncle Porter. Born on November 15, 1893, he married Laura N. Wood (born about 1897 and known as Aunt Ninny) on June 26, 1914. Porter and Laura, who was partially deaf, lived elsewhere and were not at the scene of the shooting. His younger sister Gladys was spending the night at his house, so he provided security for her and several of her friends that night. Because Porter and Laura were part of the Fryer family, they were involved in the disputes both before and after that murderous evening.

The Fryer Family Post-1915

On June 26, 1914, Porter Fryer married Laura N. Wood. By the time of the 1915 shooting, they were living in their own home on another part of the Fryer properties. Photo from the collection of Tomme Jennings.

Laura and Porter were the parents of one daughter. Maurine Fryer (1916-1981), who married V. G. "Bob" Warner of New Orleans. Their daughter, Debra Frances Warner, was the President of the New Orleans Chapter and State Director of The National Association of Independent Appraisers, a three-time President of the Auction Bureau of New Orleans, and was considered one of the first females to cry at an auction in the South. Bob died in 1976 and Maurine passed away on October 1, 1981. Both are interred at the Hope Mausoleum in New Orleans, Louisiana.

Rock was an iron worker and worked on building the Main Street and Broadway bridges over the Arkansas River at Little Rock. He then moved about the country building bridges and similar structures. He was a member of the Iron Workers Union and census records show him living in Lorain, Ohio, in 1940, and New Orleans, Louisiana, by the mid-1950s. When Porter died on December 9, 1973, his obituary stated that he was a native of Little Rock and a resident of New Orleans. He was interred at Lake Lawn Mausoleum, located in the Lake Lawn Park Cemetery adjacent to Metairie Cemetery at New Orleans.

Porter was a skilled steel worker who worked on structures around the world. This photo shows him with his sister Maye, his wife Laura, and his daughter Maurine. The photo dates from the early 1920s. Photo from the collection of Tomme Jennings.

Floy Maye Fryer (1896-1964)

Among the survivors was the center of Bell's hatred, Floy Maye Fryer. Floy Maye, known to most as simply Maye and to me as Aunt Toots, was born on January 20, 1896, as the second daughter of the Fryer family. Family stories state that Abbie was very close to Maye, and the two supported each other. Abbie was involved with her own romance and was likely happy for Maye to be involved with hers. However, by the time Maye married Sam Bell on July 31, 1913, there were concerns. Maye started reporting that Sam was beating her and Abbie and her husband Erdie offered their assistance.

"The Girls." The women in the Fryer Family were always close, and here are Maye, Abbie, Gladys and Bernice, and well as Laura, the wife of Porter. This photo was likely taken only a year or two before the shootings that killed Abbie. Photo from the collection of Tomme Jennings.

Sam Bell started threatening Abbie, stating that she and the rest of the Fryer family were trying to keep him apart from his wife. The beatings continued and several members of the Fryer family rescued Maye from Bell, and she moved back to the family farm, where she received medical treatment for her injuries. Despite the public threats, and possibly because of them, Maye divorced Bell for cruelty after seven months of marriage and "went to live with her own people." There were also accusations that Bell wasn't faithful to Maye as she reportedly acquired syphilis from him.

During the trials of 1915, Maye became the spokesman for the family, speaking out and writing several letters providing the Fryer family's version of the story. She worked with the prosecuting attorneys, often sitting with them at the trials. During this time, she also replaced her sister Abbie as the postmaster at Solgohachia.

In 1922, Maye was interviewed in response to the recapture of Sam Bell after his escape from prison. In the interview, published in the *Arkansas Gazette* (April 23, 1922), she stated that Sam Bell's temper was so unstable and so ungovernable that he could easily kill without compunction. She explained the conflict between Bell and her family, and also some of the details about the divorce.

> *My parents always treated him most kindly. But for some strange reason that he never explained to me he disliked my family, especially Abbie, the sister he killed. Two months after we married he forbade my visiting my parents, and although they lived only 14 miles away I did not enter their home again until I left him, five months later. Because he had such a violent temper my father and brother avoided him as much as they could and wouldn't go to any of*

the neighborhood gatherings if they thought he would be there. Then he went away and was gone more than a year. My father and brother did not know that he had returned until the day before they were killed. That anything my people did or said caused our divorce is false. I left him simply because I could not stand his abuse and cruel treatment.

I would greatly prefer that this matter had not been brought up again. I do not want the publicity, nor to air the old trouble again, but his intimation that my people ever treated him any way but kindly is untrue and unjust, and I made this denial in justice to their memory.

Bell claimed that the separation and divorce had damaged his reputation and that even if it took twenty years, he would kill everyone involved. For the year following the divorce, Maye was hidden from Bell. It is very possible that the reason Bell ransacked the home of Erdie and Abbie Bearden after he killed them was that he was looking for Maye.

Maye, along with much of the Fryer family, fled their home and took shelter at the houses of several neighbors. After the trial, Theresa Fryer and much of the family moved to Little Rock. There, Theresa bought a boarding house and operated it for years.

Floy Maye married Clay Chester Sisemore (1886-1961), my "Uncle Si", in 1919. They moved to Texas so that Si could conduct work in the oil fields, and later lived in Dallas (coincidentally near where Bell was captured after his escape from prison). One of Clay's primary jobs was to assist companies in closing stores or operations, and he held many "going out of business" sales and auctions across the region. Clay had previously been married to Cena Fox and had three daughters (Evadna, Geraldine, and Claysel). Clay and Cena divorced about 1918, and Cena remarried and became Cena Bennett Nelson, living in Missouri.

The three daughters all kept the Sisemore name. Evadna Sisemore (1908-1960) married Isaac Albert Gatlin, later a U.S. Army Colonel who fought in World War II and Korea. Both are buried in Section 4 of the Fort Smith National Cemetery. Geraldine Sisemore (1912-1969) was born in Watts, Oklahoma, and married Archie Ray Huffaker Sr. in 1931. They moved from Missouri to North Little Rock and eventually to Fort Worth where they are buried. Claysel Imogene Sisemore (1916-1984) married L. C. Cotham and lived near his family's home in Newport, Arkansas. They later moved to Mineola, Texas, where they are buried.

In 1919, Floy Maye Fryer married Clay Chester Sisemore, generally known in the family as Si. Photo from the collection of Tomme Jennings.

The Fryer Family Post-1915

The work of Clay Sisemore took him around large parts of the country, and the family photo album includes lots of photos of Si and Maye at a number of these places. Here they are at an unnamed location, but trying to stay dry as they cross a small stream. Photo from the collection of Tomme Jennings.

Clay and Maye had no children of their own, but they did adopt Richard Elmo Fryer, a son of James Dwight Fryer, Maye's youngest brother. Clay was known in the furniture industry, especially with his ability to develop advertising campaigns and to handle volume sales. For a number of years he partnered with William Franklin Fryer (another of Maye's brothers) in the Park Hill Furniture Company. Clay was known for coming up with the company's slogan of "We Cheat You For Less."

Despite remarrying and moving, Bell always kept track of Maye's whereabouts. For years, Sam Bell would drive to

North Little Rock and park across the street from the home of Aunt Toots and just sit in the car. With a number of family members living nearby on Park Hill, everyone was always on the lookout for Bell.

Clay Sisemore died on March 24, 1961, and was buried at Roselawn Memorial Park Cemetery in Little Rock. Almost three years later, Aunt Toots had a stroke. While unable to talk, she telephoned her sister Gladys. Gladys sensed who the caller was and walked the several blocks to Maye's house. Finding Maye in bad shape, she called an ambulance. Aunt Toots never came to and passed away on May 6, 1964, and was buried next to Clay.

Maye, like many of her immediate family, was buried in the Roselawn Memorial Park Cemetery in Little Rock, Arkansas. This stone marks her final resting place. Photo by Barton Jennings.

William Franklin Fryer (1900-1987)

William Franklin "Buddy" Fryer was my "Uncle Buddy", but was known to most as either "Jerry" or "Buddy." He was born on September 28, 1900, and was apparently one of the sons who took his mother away from the shooting. Like most of the family, he moved to Little Rock after the trial.

The 1920 census shows him living with his mother, but that he was working as a salesman at a drug store.

In 1925, Buddy married Vera Kathleen Hill, who had been born on November 8, 1897, at Decatur, Texas. They met in North Little Rock where Vera moved in 1922. Vera was only about five feet tall, and soon acquired the nicknames of BeeBe and Beeb, used mainly by the nieces and nephews in the family.

The couple had a daughter on July 26, 1926, Jerry Kathleen, later Jerry Rider. Jerry Kathleen became "Little Jerry" while Buddy became "Big Jerry." The use of Big and Little was somewhat common in the family because of the many generations of Fryers with the same names. Jerry Kathleen married Jack Rider, and like almost everyone associated with the Fryer family, the Rider family soon became a target of Sam Bell. Jack's mother Madge loved fishing, and once while fishing near Conway, Arkansas, was approached by a stranger who introduced himself as Sam Bell. He asked her if she'd ever heard of the Fryer family. Feeling that this was strange, she said no. He then said that he'd killed several people in that family. She quickly packed up and left, later getting some of the family story and a warning to never mention the event to Buddy because it made him very sad.

When the family farm property near Sologohachia was sold, Buddy insisted that the family keep the mineral rights since coal and natural gas had been found in the area. For many family members, this has been fortunate since there has been a natural gas boom in northern Conway County. Several natural gas wells are now located on the property.

Like several members of the family, Jerry worked in the furniture industry for several stores, eventually becoming the owner of the Park Hill Furniture Company (We Cheat You For Less....). The furniture store was known for its Christmas sales in July. Buddy was a true businessman who loved to negotiate and work a deal. One of my favorite stories about him was when he went to a Walmart and asked the price for a Christmas tree that was fully decorated and on display. After getting a price, he paid and then walked over, picked up the display tree, and started to walk out. When stopped, he reminded the clerk that he had specifically pointed at that tree. He got the tree and used it for years, never taking it apart or having to decorate it again.

Buddy, like many members of the Fryer family, was photographed with his car. Owning a car in those days was something to brag about. Photo from the collection of Tomme Jennings.

This photo of Buddy and Vera certainly yells 1920s.
Photo from the collection of Tomme Jennings.

Many of the members of the Fryer family traveled together for their entire lives. This photo shows Buddy, Vera, and Gladys on one of their trips to the lake. Photo from the collection of Tomme Jennings.

Jerry lived on Park Hill in North Little Rock until his death on February 12, 1987. Vera preceded him in death on March 20, 1980. Both were buried at Roselawn Memorial Park in Little Rock, near the grave of Theresa Reiter Fryer. Maye, Elmo and Gladys were also buried at Roselawn Memorial Park, known by many as Roselawn Cemetery. The cemetery dates from May 25, 1919, when plans were created for the 100-acre facility. The first burial was on February 4, 1920, and more than 22,000 burials have taken place since. Roselawn was the first perpetual care cemetery in Arkansas, and is the burial site of governors, congressmen and senators, industrialists, Congressional Medal of Honor recipients, and major league baseball players. The original office, known as "The Gatehouse," is listed on the National Register of Historic Places.

The Fryer Family Post-1915

This stone at Roselawn Memorial Park in Little Rock marks the burial site of William Franklin Fryer. Photo by Barton Jennings.

Thresa Gladys Fryer (1903-1999)

Thresa Gladys Fryer was my grandmother and was born at Solgohachia on May 12, 1903. Called "Granny" by me and my brother, and Gladys by almost everyone else, she was somewhat of a tomboy and was a noted athlete, playing sports like basketball. The night of the shooting, Gladys was at the home of her brother Porter. The family history of the Miller family states that Carmon Belle Miller was with Gladys that night, and that Gladys was scared to death Bell would come back and visit the other family homes. The Miller history also states that a local preacher happened to be there that night and made everyone feel better. However, this fear seemed to haunt Gladys for her entire life, making her very close to her surviving family. She also had a signal that she used to regularly let neighbors know that she was okay (raising a shade on a certain window), a signal she used almost to the end of her life.

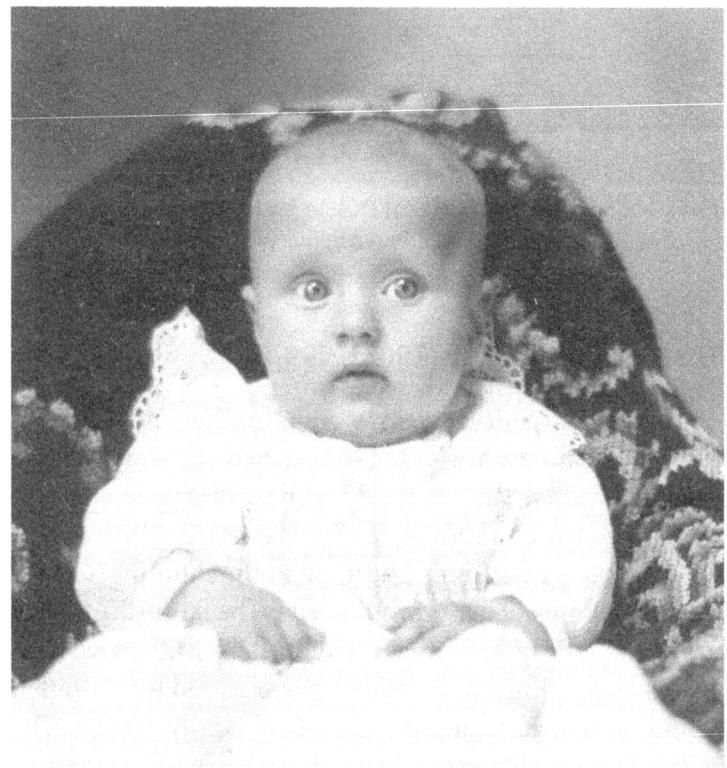

Gladys, my grandmother, was a cute baby. Photo from the collection of Tomme Jennings.

This was a high school photo of Gladys, likely during her eleventh grade as she never graduated from high school. Photo from the collection of Tomme Jennings.

Photos of my grandmother, Gladys, often show her smiling or laughing with friends. Here, she is probably joking with my grandfather, Troy Barton Wilson. Photo from the collection of Tomme Jennings.

The Fryer Family Post-1915

Speaking of jokes, this was a postcard sent to family by Gladys and Bart before they returned from a trip to Hot Springs, Arkansas. Photo from the collection of Tomme Jennings.

The family moved from Morrilton to Little Rock between Granny's 11th and 12th grade and she did not finish high school. Gladys lived with her mother until June 22, 1923, when she married Troy Barton Wilson (1901-1969) of Cave Creek, Arkansas, and then settled on Park Hill in North Little Rock during the late 1930s. There she lived within a few blocks of her brother Buddy and her sisters Floy Maye and Bernice. The Wilsons had two daughters, Billie Louise Wilson Derby (1924-2020) and Tomme Barton Wilson Jennings.

Gladys met Barton at her mother's boarding house, where he routinely ate. At the time, he was a clerk at a Piggly Wiggly grocery store and started bringing her small gifts, a habit he had with many people his entire life. In stories about these encounters, Gladys often mentioned receiving a simple banana from Barton, a story that always resulted in a smile or laugh.

Troy Barton, known as T. B. or "Big Bart", was later in the food brokerage business, working for Geyer & Adams Wholesale Grocery, and then forming his own company. He regularly traveled across several states selling goods to grocery and general stores. Gladys often traveled with "Big Bart" and I sometimes tagged along as "Little Bart". T. B. passed away in 1969 and Gladys had a say-so in how the business was managed until selling it a few years later.

Billie Louise Wilson (1924-2020), known as Sissie by some in the family, was born on April 16, 1924. During World War II, she received an offer to work at the secret Manhattan Project facilities at Oak Ridge, Tennessee, because she took chemistry in high school, but declined the opportunity. She attended Little Rock Junior College before heading to Southern Methodist University (SMU), where she entered a beauty contest. One of the judges, Cecil B. DeMille of movie fame, selected her as the winner. After college she worked as a fashion designer in Dallas with Brogan & Jennings, and some of her designs were featured in various women's magazines. On January 1, 1948, she married Rodney Welch Derby (1920-1986), another SMU student, who was originally from Denver, Colorado. Rod had been in the Air Force and was burned pretty badly in a plane crash in the States. Because of his burn scars, he was always careful in the sun. They moved to Houston where Rod worked in the auditing department at Esso, later Exxon. They had a daughter (Diane) and a son (Rod, Jr.). Rod, Sr., died in Houston, Texas, on December 1, 1986, and Billie passed away at Colorado Springs, Colorado, on January 3, 2020. Both were buried in the Memorial Mission Mausoleum at Forest Park Westheimer Cemetery in Houston.

Tomme Barton Wilson was born on April 11, 1932. The age between the two sisters was enough that Billie often did the babysitting for Tomme. After graduating high school in North Little Rock, during which she often worked at the

Park Hill Furniture Company of her uncle Buddy, she attended Hendrix College. One issue with her high school graduation was that she received a letter from the draft board at age 18. After a quick explanation that she was a girl, the matter was dropped. Upon graduation from Hendrix, Tomme was awarded The Arkansas Experiment in Teacher Education award sponsored by the Ford Foundation. This scholarship paid for all expenses except for 6 hours to get a Masters degree, plus some living expenses. She did her practice teaching at Bauxite, Arkansas, a World War II boom town due to the government's need for the local bauxite ore to make aluminum. A favorite story from the time was that she lived in the Bauxite teacherage with another student in the program. They had an ice box and had to go to the company store to get ice for it. They took a broom, walked down the railroad tracks to the store and put the broom handle through the rope on the ice and walked back down the tracks to their apartment.

While at the University of Arkansas, Tomme met Leo Jennings (1930-2020), who was in the U.S. Air Force, and later in the U.S. Navy. They married in 1956. At the time you had to have a blood test to get married, and with Leo scheduled to be away until the weekend before the wedding, Tomme warned the doctor if he broke that blood sample, he had to give his own. Leo later worked for Arkansas Power & Light/Entergy, while Tomme was a elementary school teacher and librarian. They had two children, Barton and Donald. Tomme is my mother and the source of many of the family stories and photographs.

Granny helped raise me and was at our house almost daily doing laundry and other small tasks. Meanwhile, I would visit her house almost weekly to mow and do some small chores. She moved to Springdale, Arkansas, during the mid-1990s to be near my parents, and passed away there on February 10, 1999. She and her husband are buried at Roselawn Memorial Park at Little Rock.

My grandmother, Gladys Fryer Wilson, was buried at Roselawn Memorial Park near many of her family members. Photo by Barton Jennings

Willie Bernice Fryer (1905-2001)

Willie Bernice Fryer was my "Aunt Johny" (also Aunt Johnnie) and was very close to Gladys. Known by most as Bernice, she was born on December 15, 1905. She followed her mother to Morrilton and then to Little Rock before marrying Robert Guy Finnegan (1907-1983) in 1926. My "Uncle Bob", Robert Finnegan came from Du Quoin, Illinois, and sometimes stood out at family gatherings due to his lack of a Solgohachia accent. He was a pharmacist who had a fascination with alcohol stills and small steam engines. R. G. first sold pharmaceuticals and then became a pharmacist and worked at several stores. He later owned and operated Finnegan's Highland Pharmacy in Little Rock. In 1959, Uncle Bob made the national news when he worked with law enforcement officials to arrest a "narcotics suspect" who was traveling the country illegally acquiring various narcotics and selling them through the black market.

During the 1920s, shorter hair became popular with women, especially with the fame of Amelia Earhart and her hairstyle. Bernice Fryer followed the trend, as shown in this photo. She generally kept her hair short her entire life. Photo from the collection of Tomme Jennings.

Bernice and Bob lived in North Little Rock and were regular visitors with other family members in the area. They also traveled heavily, including a drive to Alaska soon after the Alcan Highway opened, and a visit to the Florida Everglades not long after the national park was dedicated in 1934. During that visit, they were given an alligator, which they later donated to the Little Rock Zoo. Their son, Robert Franklin Finnegan (Bobby Frank), graduated from the University of Arkansas College of Medicine and became a doctor and performed a great deal of anesthetics and pain care.

A favorite family tale is that when Bob closed his pharmacy, he posted a list of items that were for sale. One of these items was a still, once used to manufacture alcohol and drugs for his pharmacy. Apparently, someone from the FBI showed up to examine the still, stating that it was illegal to sell it.

This photo is of Bernice and Bob, who remained married for more than five decades. Photo from the collection of Tomme Jennings.

The Fryer Family Post-1915

For years, Bernice and Gladys shopped and dined together. After Bob passed away in 1983, Bernice continued to travel and eventually moved to Lawton, Oklahoma, to be near her son. She passed away there on May 6, 2001, and was interred with Bob at Rest Hills Memorial Park at North Little Rock, Arkansas.

Bernice and Bob were buried side-by-side at Rest Hills Memorial Park at North Little Rock, Arkansas. Photo by Barton Jennings.

James Dwight Fryer (1908-1974)

James Dwight Fryer, known as "Uncle Dwight", was born on August 9, 1908. He was one of the children that were sent to hide in the nearby fields the night of the shooting. Like several members of the family, Dwight never seemed to get over the horror of the shooting, which took place when he was only six years old. On August 17, 1926, he married Dorothy Dee Gorham (1911-1952) of Wallaceburg, Arkansas. They were both young (Dwight had just turned 18 the week before and Dorothy was only 14) when they married, and they had four children within a few years: Wallace (1927-1997), Richard (1928-2018), Marjorie (1931-2014), and Stephen (1933-1936). They were living in Little Rock at the time of their marriage. Both Dwight and Dorothy were apparently alcoholics and showed signs of violence. During the mid-1930s, Dwight and Dorothy deserted the children and drove off to Florida. No one knew this until a few days later when a neighbor stopped by. They found Wally (Wallace) managing the kids and trying to heat a bottle for Stevie.

Mammaw Fryer was close to her children and was often photographed with them. Here she is shown with Dwight, one of her youngest children. Photo from the collection of Tomme Jennings.

The children were unfortunately split up. Wallace "Wally" Dwight Fryer was taken in by his grandmother, Theresa Reiter Fryer, and lived at the Little Rock boarding house before the family moved to the North Little Rock area. Richard "Dick" Elmo Fryer lived with Clay Chester and Floy Mae Sisemore, and asked to be adopted when he joined the military so that he could no longer use the name Fryer. Dick was part of the 7th Calvary Regiment, 191st Division during the Korean War, and later lived in Tennessee. Wally and Dick were part of a youth group that performed water shows at the pool at Fair Park in Little Rock. Wally performed classic dives while Dick was a clown.

Marjorie (Margie, often simply called Sister), was taken in by her grandmother, Ethel "Mittie" Stephens Gorham. Margie had polio and her left leg was thinner and shorter than her right. However, she could still outrun many of the other children. She was later raised by Richard E. and Gradelle Emerson Payer, whom she claimed as her parents, and moved with them to Stuttgart, Arkansas. She married Forrest M. Marchand, who passed away in 1985. She then married Edward Whelan Miller, who passed away in 2008. Known as Margie Miller, she died on November 5, 2014. All are buried at the Lone Tree Cemetery at Stuttgart.

The youngest of the children, Stephen R. Fryer, was sent to the St. Joseph's Orphanage near North Little Rock, where he was reportedly spoiled by the nuns. The orphanage was commissioned by Bishop John Morris in 1908 to house and care for orphaned and abandoned children, and was run by the Benedictine Sisters of St. Scholastica. At the time, Aunt Johny and Uncle Bob were living in a room at the back on the first floor of Mammaw's boarding house in Little Rock. They brought Stevie "home" on weekends and were talking about adopting him.

However, Stevie died in September 1936 of what was described as "The Summer Complaint," and was interred at Mount Holly Cemetery in Little Rock. The Summer Complaint was a common cause of death for young children at the time. Nicknamed "disease of the season," it seemed to come from the use of unpasteurized cow's milk and/or unfiltered water, contaminated under the excessive heat of the summer months. Scientific studies conducted in the early 1900s determined that women who continued to breast feed rarely had infants who contracted The Summer Complaint.

The summer of 1936 was the hottest summer on record in much of the United States, and one of the most severe heat waves in the modern history of North America. On June 20th, Arkansas set an all-time, monthly record high, and it only got hotter. Little Rock reached 105°F, and then Fort Smith hit 106°F on July 13th. August became the hottest month on record for Arkansas, with 120°F being recorded in Ozark. The average temperature was 4.1°F above average and there was only 0.27" of rain. More than 5000 people across the country died from heat stroke and heat exhaustion, and many others died from heat-related illnesses like The Summer Complaint.

In some ways, the abandonment of the children was Stephen's death sentence. Hearing these details, one Fryer family member wrote: "What a family we come from! It was the tragedy that just kept giving."

The sign over the entrance to St. Joseph's Orphanage near North Little Rock. Photo by Barton Jennings.

Dwight and Dorothy eventually broke up and Dorothy returned to her family who were living near McCaskill, in southwest Arkansas. She passed away there and was buried in the nearby Friendship Cemetery at McCaskill in 1952. In spite of everything, her grave marker still shows the name Dorothy Gorham Fryer.

Like his younger brother Richard Elmo, who Dwight named his second son for, Dwight's drinking problem controlled much of his life. However, he sobered up and reportedly never drank again when he heard of his brother's death from alcoholism in 1946. James Dwight Fryer later worked as a butcher near Memphis, Tennessee, where he passed away on January 15, 1974. He was buried in Covington, Tennessee.

Richard Elmo Fryer (1911-1946)

Richard Elmo Fryer was the youngest of the Fryer children. Later a Second Lieutenant in the U.S. Army, Richard Elmo Fryer was a boxer and army infantry officer who died from alcohol abuse, which caused a disease of the kidneys and congestion of his lungs. "Uncle Elmo" was born on April 16, 1911, and was barely four years old when the shootings occurred. He was a noted athlete at Little Rock Eastside Junior High School, a trend that continued through college. In the 1930 census, he was shown to be the only child of Theresa and Dick to still be living at home.

Elmo later attended Georgia Tech where he was a member of the school's boxing team. He was mentioned frequently in an article about the boxing team in the February 1932 issue of the *Georgia Tech Alumni Magazine*. At the time Elmo was in training for the 1932 Los Angeles Summer Olympics as a welterweight. He didn't make the team, but American Edward Flynn did win the gold medal in that weight class. Elmo later participated in the 1933 national amateur boxing tournament.

By 1940, Elmo was a resident of Washington, D.C., and then fought in World War II. The war and his family history were hard on Elmo, and he had developed a drinking habit by this time. After the war, he was admitted to the U.S. Veterans Administration medical center at Fort Logan H. Roots in North Little Rock, Arkansas. He died from his "long standing" kidney condition, plus congestion of his lungs, at 5:40am on February 22, 1946. He was buried at Roselawn Memorial Park in Little Rock, next to where his mother would be buried. It should be noted that his cemetery marker shows his date of death as February 26, 1946, while a letter from the hospital used a February 22nd date.

This is a high school photo of Elmo Fryer. Photo from the collection of Tomme Jennings.

The Fryer Family Post-1915

This photo shows Elmo Fryer near his 30th birthday. Note the receding hairline, a trait of the family. Photo from the collection of Tomme Jennings.

During World War II, Elmo served in the military, as shown in this informal photo. Photo from the collection of Tomme Jennings.

The Solgohachia Murders

In various family photo albums, Elmo was commonly photographed with his mother, Theresa Reiter Fryer. It is appropriate that he was buried by her side in Little Rock, Arkansas. Photo from the collection of Tomme Jennings.

Second Lieutenant Richard Elmo Fryer was the first of the Solgohachia survivors to pass away, apparently broken by the family tragedy and then his military experience in World War II. He was buried in Roselawn Memorial Park in Little Rock, with his mother buried next to him ten years later. Photo by Barton Jennings.

Lloyd? Who was Lloyd?

> Mrs. Fryer, attracted by the shooting and failure to learn the whereabouts of her husband and son, left her home. She proceeded only a short distance along the road when overtaken by two sons. The elder one stopped her and started to run along the road, carrying her back toward home. Bell saw the trio. He fired his eighth shot. But the distance was too great. The shot only sprinkled Lloyd Fryer, who continued carrying his mother to J. M. Atkinson's house. Mr. Atkinson assisted the youth to carry Mrs. Fryer to the second story of the house. There, with the surviving members of her family, she spent the night unaware of the fate of her daughter, her husband, her son and her son-in-law.

Arkansas Gazette
Wednesday, April 28, 1915

A number of early newspaper reports about the murders of the Fryer and Bearden families cited a Lloyd Fryer as carrying Theresa Fryer from the scene. However, the Fryer family and various census reports have no record of anyone named Lloyd. There are a few clues as to who the person was. Probably the most important one is that "Lloyd" was the elder brother, however the Bearden history of the shooting lists Lloyd as one of the youngest boys.

If "Lloyd" was the oldest brother, then he was really Roy Thomas Fryer. Based upon the Bearden history, he was William Franklin Fryer. Neither were known to ever use the name Lloyd. However, there might be a simple reason for this name problem. The first newspaper reports stated that they had been received by telephone from Morrilton.

At the time, telephone connections were not always clear and it is possible that the name Roy was mistaken as being Lloyd. Additionally, the Little Rock newspapers generally led the story reporting, which was copied by other newspapers. Therefore, a simple error during the confusion of the first minutes after the shootings probably created "Lloyd Fryer".

However, *The Log Cabin Democrat* of Conway County seemed to have gotten it correct in an article in their Tuesday, April 27, 1915, edition. It stated that "Roy Fryer was fired upon by Bell, but the shot missed him."

The Missing

These brief histories of the surviving members of the Fryer family and their descendants makes one wonder what could have been if not for that fateful night in April 1915.

About the Author

Barton Jennings grew up in Arkansas, including many years in the North Little Rock area where he got to know many members of the Fryer family, relatives on his mother's side of the family. However, during this time, he seldom heard any mention of the events of April 26, 1915, although he knew many of those who were there. It was only decades later that a few photos and the comments of his mother led him to begin to research the event.

"Little Bart" obtained several engineering degrees and worked in the railroad industry before taking on a teaching career at the university level. There he taught railroad engineering and operations, transportation management, and a field that became known as supply chain management. This work, and his PhD from the University of Tennessee, taught him a number of research techniques, many used in researching the events at Solgohachia.

Today, Barton Jennings, after years working in the railroad and teaching industries, is a professor emeritus of supply chain management and still teaches transportation operations part-time. He also still teaches regulatory issues for the railroad industry, a way to stay in touch with the industry he loves. He is the author of a number of transportation books in the *History Through the Miles* series, plus the textbook *The Basics of Transportation: Policies, Practices and Pricing – an Applied Perspective*.

The author at the Solgohachia Friendship Community Cemetery. Photo by Sarah Jennings.

www.ingramcontent.com/pod-product-compliance
Lightning Source LLC
Chambersburg PA
CBHW060505030426
42337CB00015B/1751